SPIRITUA

A personal account of the healing
author shows that healing is not a
everyone.

SPIRITUAL HEALING
The Power of the Gentle Touch

by
The Rev. Dudley Blades

THE AQUARIAN PRESS
Wellingborough, Northamptonshire

First published 1979
Second Impression 1981
Third Impression 1982
Fourth Impression 1984
Fifth Impression 1986

ISBN 0 85030 130 0

Printed and bound in Great Britain

To 'Jamie'

CONTENTS

INTRODUCTION

So – for some reason or other you have bought or borrowed this book, and you are now glancing at the introduction to see what it is all about.

Does the title intrigue you? What does the word healing mean to you? The supernatural, the miraculous, the cranky world of those who will believe anything?

Why am I asking these questions? I cannot hear your answers. The point is, is it going to be worth your while to read and to study this little book? The best way for me to help you to make that decision is to give you some idea of the sort of person I had in mind when I was putting this book together.

Let's begin by imagining a person who is interested in people. I know that in some way or other almost everybody is interested in people, but there are some whose motive for being interested would disqualify them as possible readers of this book. The hard-sell salesman who sees people only as potential customers and who only forms relationships on the basis of what he can get out of it. You do not actually have to be a salesman to look upon your brothers and sisters in the human family as objects to be manipulated in some way or other. There are those whose sole use for others is to be an audience for their opinions, grumbles, and what have you, and we have all met the type who looks at others only to see the worst in them.

Being interested in people, in my definition, means being concerned for the well-being of others, having compassion, to use an old-fashioned but not outmoded word. Being ready to help when help is needed. Being concerned when things go ill with them and glad when things go well.

I also had in mind someone who was interested in life. In the meaning of life. What is life all about? Why are we here? And what about death?

There will also be an interest in what is often called religion. By this I mean something other than going to church or being a member of some denomination or sect. The vast majority of people in Great Britain do not go to church and do not claim active membership of a religious organization, yet they are likely to have thoughts, views and questions of a religious, or as I would prefer to say, of a spiritual nature. Mind you, I am not ruling out members of churches. As a minister myself it grieves me that healing has been neglected and ignored by church folk for so long.

Interest is growing, of course, but one gets the impression that there is greater interest, not only in healing but in other spiritual matters, being shown by the majority outside the organized religions than from those within the ranks. There are some movements that place healing very firmly in a place of prominence within their activities. The Spiritualist Association and Christian Science are probably the best known examples.

This brings me to the third and most important quality which I had in mind. It is best described as open-mindedness, a willingness to listen to the opinions and experiences of others, being open to new ideas, being interested in truth and not prejudging any issue with an attitude of 'As we are right then everyone else must be wrong'.

So, if you are interested in people, in life, and are open-minded, yes, this book is for you.

Something About Myself

Now let me tell you something about myself, who I am and how I came to write this book. I want to begin at a time, in my early twenties, when I was a policeman. I wore the number 110 on my shoulders and the badge of Tynemouth Borough Police on my helmet. I still have both, as souvenirs of those days.

An interest in the church had developed over the previous five or six years, in my case the Presbyterian Church of England, and the focus of my interest was the Presbyterian Fellowship of Youth, a national organization that was remarkable in many ways, not least in its age range of seventeen to thirty. In the summer of 1957 I was at a Summer Conference of the F.O.Y., as we called it. Dr William Barclay was the speaker and in his own forceful and authoritative way he delved into the Gospels and showed us Jesus.

It was the practice for certain individuals, usually group leaders or committee members, to lead the evening prayers and it was my turn on the Monday night. My plans for this included a short address and this was carefully written out, word for word, on about four pieces of paper and carefully placed in order ready to hand. After a hymn and a prayer I took up these pieces of paper and found that they were hopelessly jumbled up. I think I panicked for a moment, everyone was waiting for me to say something, so I began to speak 'off the top of my head'. Afterwards I hadn't the faintest recollection of what I had said but William Barclay came straight up to me, shook my hand and said, in his rich Scottish accent, 'Well done, it was worth coming south just to hear that.'

I was shaken by both aspects of this experience, but more was to come. For some time there had been the feeling at the back of my mind that I would like to be a minister, but it was out of the question of course. The Presbyterian Church of England demanded high academic standards of its ministers and I had left school at fourteen. Besides, I had a widowed mother to support. A further complication was a speech impediment. This was not insuperable, although subsequently a member of the ministerial students selection board voted against me because of it. However, the events of that week were proceeding. Unknown to me my mother had been taken ill and friends were trying to contact me. The police were called in to help and on the Wednesday morning I received the message, 'Go home immediately, mother seriously ill'. The conference was being held at Keele University and I don't know how many times I changed trains before reaching Newcastle Central Station on Tyneside. I eventually arrived home at seven o'clock in the evening, my mother spoke to me and died at ten minutes past seven.

The story of that evening has been told many times since. There was an unseen presence in the room. In my naive way I identified it as Jesus. Some words from St John's Gospel came to mind: 'I go to prepare a place for you. I will come again and receive you unto myself, that where I am ye may be also.' Jesus, I thought, has come to take mum home.

I was happy, uplifted, humble and oh, all sorts of other things as well, but to cut a long story short, on that night I decided to offer myself for the ministry. Dimly I could see a connection between the events of the Monday and Wednesday evenings. The connection was strong enough: it was the understanding of it that was dim – or maybe I was.

I was aware that the supernatural had impinged on my life and I think that I have a greater understanding of it all now than I had then. Destiny is a word with many meanings but I can now see that I was being guided, pushed, the polite word in church circles is 'called', to follow a certain path.

Time passed. In the mid 1960s I was ordained and went to my first church, in my own county of Northumberland, a village in North Tynedale called Bellingham, pronounced 'Bell-in-jim' after the Northumbrian fashion.

I became interested in clinical theology, a mixture of psychology and religion, very useful in understanding mental illnesses. This interest was shared by my Anglican colleagues in the village, Bernard Garman and his successor, Geoffrey Charles. It was the latter who once mentioned a book on healing. *The Forgotten Talent* by a Scottish Presbyterian minister, James Cameron Peddie. I should have tried to get hold of a copy – but I didn't.

Another few years passed. I moved to Salford and one Sunday morning those who had been pushing or guiding me achieved a breakthrough. A lady member of my church, Kathie, asked me if I knew anything about healing. My answer was no but I was interested. It turned out that two fellows, Ken and Edmund, had been visiting her, giving her healing. Two years previously she had been in a wheelchair, with disseminated sclerosis, I think, and now she was so much better that she was learning to play tennis again. I said that I would be interested in meeting these two – and that was the beginning of my direct involvement in spiritual healing. Ken and Edmund were spiritualists, with a small 's', and their talk of spirit guides worried me a little. The mainstream Christian churches have long been suspicious of spiritualism, and still are to some extent.

After that, everywhere I turned I was met with healing in one way or another: articles in papers and magazines, talks on radio and on television. Every book in the library seemed to be on healing.

I visited a friend that Christmas and sitting in an armchair next to a bookcase I idly glanced at some of the books. One leapt out at me: *The Forgotten Talent*, the book I should have read four years earlier. A book that tells of how the Rev. Peddie discovered healing and of the wonders of his healing ministry. I took that book and devoured it. It took Peddie fifteen years to get started and I remember thinking what a lot of time he had wasted. It is only since I have been writing this that I have realized, with a terrible sinking feeling, that it is twenty years since that week at conference with William Barclay!

Those who had been guiding me had shown marvellous patience as I failed to see the significance of a whole series of events, many more than I have mentioned here. For I too am now convinced of the presence in my life of those whom the church may call 'the faithful departed', what the Bible may call 'The unseen cloud of witnesses', and what spiritualists certainly call 'guides'. To me they are people, friends, and together we co-operate in the ministry of healing.

How different things could have been if someone had been on hand twenty years ago to explain what was happening. What a lot could have been done in that time. Let my story be a warning to you. It may not be idle chance that has brought this book into your hands. There may be a healing ministry for *you* and a pattern of golden clues scattered along the pathway of your years and trodden underfoot as you passed by.

1

THE TRUTH ABOUT HEALING

The purpose of this chapter is to de-mythologize healing. De-mythologizing is an attempt to strip away the myths which surround a subject, in order to reveal or lay bare the truth of the matter. Some theologians seek to de-mythologize beliefs about God, much to the annoyance of other theologians, and, to be fair, the results are generally uncomfortable. We remember the Bishop of Woolwich's book, *Honest to God* and Professor Hick's *The Myth of God Incarnate*. In the long run the de-mythologizers seem to win the day, even if it is only in the sense that things are never quite the same again.

'I Haven't the Gift'
In church circles the subject of healing has attracted its fair share of myths, clinging like barnacles to the bottom of a ship, hiding the shining truth. 'I haven't got the gift of healing' is one such myth. That was the reply of a minister, a colleague of mine, when I broached the subject to him. Others have echoed his words and I get the impression that the majority of clergymen would agree, however much they regret it, that the gift of healing has not come their way. Their regret is usually genuine. They read the healing stories in the gospels, they hear of modern 'miracles' and they sigh and say, 'Wouldn't it be wonderful if I could put my hands on someone who was sick – and cure them? But, alas, I haven't got the gift.' The trouble is, you see, that they have been brainwashed into believing that healing *is* a gift, when it is nothing of the sort. St Paul is at the root of this trouble. He gave a list of spiritual gifts, but that list also includes preaching, which is

something that most parsons do quite a lot. How many of them would honestly claim to have the 'gift' of preaching? There was a time when I wished that I was a gifted preacher, one who could get results, fill the empty pews and – well, we all dream, don't we? I fancy that there are not many preachers today with 'the gift'. Yet they all do it. At college they studied it, they read about it, they talked about it. Long hours were spent in preparing sermons and ever since they were ordained they have done it. Sunday after Sunday they have preached. Perhaps over the years they have got better at it, perhaps they have seen results, whatever that may mean. Perhaps if they were asked why they preached they might say, 'It is part of my ministry', and quote the commission of Jesus, 'Preach the gospel'. But that quotation goes on, 'Heal the sick'. Healing is also part of the ministry, and should be approached in the same way as preaching. Study healing, talk about it, read about, but above all, *do* it. Far from being a gift, healing is an art, a craft, a science. There is an apprenticeship to be served and a Master to serve under. How dare you even think that the ability will suddenly be dropped into your lap, as some kind of special favour?

Well now, having had a 'go' at my fellow ministers, having conveniently forgotten my wasted years, let it be said that of the many thousands of men and women who are engaged in healing in Britain, very few of them are ordained ministers. It is predominantly a lay craft. Why should this be so? Well, there may be many reasons but one of them is that, for many people, an interest in healing develops when they have been on the receiving end, as it were. Having experienced what healing can do for them, they start asking questions, perhaps beginning with, 'How does healing work?' and ending with, 'Could I become a healer?'

A large part of this book is devoted to answering the first question, but the second can be answered very shortly. The answer is, yes, you could become a healer. Anybody can give healing, if they wish.

Another Myth

Another of the myths that cling to the subject of healing states that although much healing was done by Jesus and the disciples, this being God's love at work, times have changed and nowadays God's healing work is done through doctors and nurses, i.e., through the medical profession.

I must admit that I have not heard this said recently, but it was once so common as to be almost an official line of the Church. On the surface it is a persuasive argument, simply because there is a certain amount of truth in it.

I certainly believe that all healing work is divinely blessed, although I would prefer to use the word spiritually, but it is quite another thing to say that all the healing eggs are in the one basket.

The argument is purely a get-out, a face-saving answer to the awkward question, 'Why are there no healing "miracles" in Christianity today, when there seemed to be so many in the beginning?' No churchman who was involved in healing would give such an unsatisfactory answer. Mind you, in one sense it is true that the age of miracles has passed. Miracle is a word that was conveniently used to label events that were not understood. Today we know a lot about the natural laws that govern sickness and health. Today we know that spiritual healing is a natural process and while we are pleased when a course of treatment goes according to plan, and disappointed when it does not, at least we realize that there is a plan. The word miracle has out-lived its usefulness. Indeed the main users of it today seem to be journalists who one week may be reporting a 'miracle cure' at the hands of a 'faith-healer' and the next week announcing another 'miracle of modern science'. There is also a certain amount of mythology regarding the history of healing. I suppose it is natural, in a society like ours with a strong Christian culture, to presume that healing began in Galilee with the coming of Jesus. This is not the case.

Healing in Ancient Egypt
Many ancient civilizations were more spiritually developed than the Israel of 2000 years ago, and wherever there was a high level of spirituality there was also healing. In some ways the ancient Egyptians may claim pre-eminence in the healing arts. With no division between religion and medicine, temples of healing were an accepted part of the culture. If an operation was necessary, probably using bronze scalpels, an essential member of the operating team would be the Ka priest who would lead the Ka or spirit of the patient out of his body, and keep it out so that no pain or shock was felt. We might prefer to call this hypnotism and say that such a thing could happen today. True enough, but it couldn't have happened in the England of two hundred years ago. The ancient Egyptians were certainly more advanced in these matters than we were in the eighteenth century. If their 'trance' method of anaesthetization was used in childbirth, which it is possible it was, then they were also more understanding and compassionate than nineteenth-century Christian Church leaders in Britain who stoutly maintained that it was ordained that childbirth should be painful.

Another important facet of ancient Egyptian medicine was colour healing. This is another of those aspects that is being discovered afresh in our time, although it is a long way from being fully understood or accepted. Picture in your mind a series of rooms within the precincts of a temple beside the banks of the Nile. The sunlight streams through the glass windows to light up these rooms, but the windows are glazed with coloured glass. One room, think of them as private wards if you like, has blue windows, and the bright sun is filtered, bathing that room with a quiet blue that is very peaceful to anyone who has to spend some time there. In another room the glazing passes red rays, in another green, and so on. Each room, bathed in a different colour, is used for healing. Blue for someone who is anxious or worried, red for someone who is physically weak and needs strength.

The important principle behind this use of light is that all spiritual healing is carried out in this way. This should come as no surprise to our twentieth-century minds. Ultra-violet rays and infra-red rays are well known for their beneficial effects and thousands of heat-lamps and sun-lamps are in daily use. What may be surprising is that all the visible rays of the spectrum, visible, that is, in a rainbow, have particular and valuable contributions to make towards healing and the maintenance of health. Indeed many more than these seven are used, and I well remember the beauty of seeing amethyst rays dancing around the head and shoulders of someone I was giving healing to. We shall go deeper into this later on, the point that we are making at the moment is that the Egyptians of long ago had knowledge that our Western world is only just coming to. And not only the Egyptians, the Chinese of 4500 years ago probably knew as much about our common illnesses as we know today.

The Gospel Healing Stories

In the Israel of 2000 years ago healers were not uncommon, Jesus and the disciples did not start something new – although it may be argued that they did it better! New Testament healing stories are usually of the instantaneous kind and this again can be something of a problem. Why doesn't that sort of thing happen nowadays? Let us spend some time on that.

First we need to look at the way in which the healing stories were included in a gospel. Imagine that you are writing a life of Jesus. Your first problem concerns your writing material, a length of papyrus. Papyrus was made from the pith of reeds, flattened into strips about one and a half to two inches wide. The strips were laid out, overlapping each other, and pressed and ironed into a long length. The top surface would be smoothed to take writing and the length rolled up, rather like a roll of heavy duty wallpaper. Because of weight, bulk and the fragile nature of papyrus, there was a limit to the length of scroll that it was practicable to use.

The second problem would be that there was more material in the way of stories, anecdotes, quotations, etc., than the gospel writer had room for. He would need to be selective. St John's gospel refers to this. The very last verse of that gospel reads, 'But there are also many other things that Jesus did; were every one of them to be written, I suppose that the world itself could not contain the books that would be written.' In particular there must have been hundreds of healing stories, and the gospel writer could only include a dozen or so. How did he make his selection? Well, we do not know. Perhaps he highlighted the different types of illnesses that were tackled, or perhaps he selected the most impressive cures, the 'instant' cures.

On the other hand we have to bear in mind the natures of the people involved, both the healer and the recipient.

A healer is a channel for spiritual power. The better the channel, the more power can pass through. When we talk of Jesus we are speaking of one who obviously was capable of giving the fullest expression to the power of the spirit and, other things being equal, could bring about a swifter cure, if a quick cure was what was best for the patient. There is an important principle here that we shall come back to later. The attitude of the seeker is also important in analyzing the gospel healing stories.

A Personal Experience

Most of the seekers in the Gospels expected to get better or believed that they would recover. In our healing work we are likely to be faced with a certain amount of reservation or even scepticism. At the very least this will slow down the effects of healing. Again we must say that this will be dealt with more fully later on in the book; it is sufficient for the moment to say that anyone taking up healing should not expect that in a short while they will be seeing instantaneous cures, 'just like the Bible'.

And yet the healing life is full of surprises. I used to get occasional visits from an African, a native of Gambia, Abdul by name. He was the son of a witch-doctor and has since gone back home to take up the family business, as one might say. Although he had inherited a lot of psychic powers (as we would call them), such as clairvoyance and psychometry, they were not very effective in this country. A mixture of cultures is never satisfactory, and Abdul, a Muslim, used to come to me for help.

He called to see me one day after he had been involved in a car accident. By all accounts he had had a lucky escape. The front passenger seat is no place to be when a car crashes into a wall. However, he had taken a heavy knock on the side of his head. His left cheek was bruised and swollen and he had difficulty in talking. He could not see out of his left eye, though this was not because of the swelling but was due to internal damage. He also had a severe headache.

When he told me all this I offered to give him some healing. This surprised him because he hadn't previously known that I did healing, but he agreed readily enough. I stood behind the chair on which he was sitting and put my hands on his head. Within a few seconds he said that the headache was going. After a few more seconds he could see again out of his left eye and after half a minute all his pain had gone. He was amazed at the change and jumped up, thumping his cheek with his clenched fist to show me that it was all gone. This worried me more than a little and I had to stop him doing that in case it all came back!

I have never, before or since, seen such a swift transformation – half a minute from beginning to end.

Why did it happen so quickly? Was it because he was African? A Muslim? A witch-doctor? I do not know the reason but I tell the story to indicate that the recipient can help or hinder the healing process. My part in that affair was probably no different from many other similar incidents but the results were certainly not typical, indeed they were quite unlike any other reaction in their swiftness or completeness, for Abdul had no recurrence of any of the symptoms.

It would be possible for me to fill the rest of this book with stories of healing, case histories if you like, but if I were to do this I think you would soon grow tired of reading them. Some will be mentioned of course, to illustrate a point, but the most important avenue to explore is that which leads us to an understanding of what healing is, how it works, or does not work. How the healing power can be used and how it should not be used. It will be seen as we progress that we have to make many diversions, in order to clear away misconceptions that are obstacles in our path.

2

THE SOURCE OF HEALING POWER

Just what is the power that heals? The short answer is that it is of God. It is God who heals. But, and here is our first diversion, that short answer may conjure up in your mind a picture of God as a sort of human figure stretching forth his hand in healing. Any such anthropomorphic picture is not helpful at this stage. Once again it may be useful to go back to ancient cultures, to sun worshippers, for example. Our Christian culture has perhaps left us with the impression that all such were 'pagans' who did not understand the true nature of God. In fact the boot may be on the other foot.

The Analogy of the Sun

Try to consider, in an abstract sort of way, what the sun does. It is creative in that it brings forth life. Nothing can grow without the warming rays of the sun's light. See how a flower opens up to the light, follows it round the sky then closes as the sun sets. The sun is the prime source of light and energy. It was eminently sensible of those 'pagans' to worship the sun and the only real objection to such worship is that the sun is impersonal, natural, and just one aspect of a much larger creation. In its own way it may be a bringer of life to that which lies dormant, but it does not of itself create life being itself created.

Fair enough; but we do an injustice to our sun worshippers. For the physical sun was to them largely symbolic. What they worshipped was the spirit behind the sun. The sun which traversed the daily sky was used as a vehicle, a chariot perhaps, by the spiritual sun which was the real creator God who used the rays of the physical sun to carry his creative blessings to earth. In fact they worshipped Spirit and Light and would find no fault with New Testament statements such as, 'God is spirit' and 'I am the light of the world'.

While they may have lacked the personal side of God which Christians find so important, it is also true that we lack the impersonal, natural side of God. I am sure that a lot of people find it difficult to understand how God, a personal God, can be in two places at once. They probably give up when asked to believe that God is everywhere! I think it was Carl Jung who said that if the Divine Spark was in man, it was also in every tree, every blade of grass and every mountain stream. An echo perhaps of St John's gospel which says of the Logos, 'All that came to be was alive with his life'.

Divine Energy

What we need to understand is that the whole of creation is full of divine energy, divine power, the very stuff of life. The power which is used in healing fills the universe and is a natural manifestation of the divine. That which enables good wholesome tissue to grow and to continue to grow; that which is constantly replacing dead matter with new matter – the divine energy. Orientals call it Prana and identify this with the creative Logos of St John's gospel. Prana, they say, is everywhere, it is in the air but it is not air, it is in water but it is not water. Hatha Yoga teaches that the way to maintain good health involves breathing properly, filling the lungs and accumulating a reserve of Prana from the inexhaustible store that surrounds us.

We need to remember that the world, by which I mean everything that is alive, is constantly in a state of change and replacement. That goes for our bodies too. Cell replacement goes on, at a fantastic rate, in every part of our system. Nearly every cell that dies is immediately replaced with an exact copy. New cells for old, in a wonderful complexity that nevertheless works on a principle of harmony and unity between the many parts. Blood cells do not replace skin cells, neither do bone cells replace blood cells. The guiding intelligence behind it all, more wonderful than any computer, is the divine spark within us, our spirit, itself part of, and in harmony with, *The Spirit*, God. It has been truly said that man is a microcosm of the macrocosm.

The main cause of illness is a deficiency in our input of divine energy, or as the Hindus would say, prana-starvation. Perhaps the best illustration of this is to imagine a miner, pot-holer or fireman who spends too much time where the air is bad. The cell replacement programme is immediately affected, notably in the blood and the brain. He needs extra oxygen to restore harmony. My own way of putting it is to say that a person's spiritual batteries are run down, and I often give someone a little healing just to recharge their batteries. Anyone who is engaged in healing is able to do this, giving spiritual energy, either from his own store or from 'outside'. A healer is, after all, only a channel, a pipeline, for the passage of spiritual energy. In the early days, before the channel is really open, a healer is apt to be tapping his own resources every time. This is why beginners sometimes feel drained after they have given healing. This stage is soon passed, in a matter of weeks perhaps, as the channel is widened and he is able to draw more on outside supplies.

One more thought on natural sources of healing power before we pass on. The sun is the main bringer of natural, divine, spiritual power, and each of us should endeavour to spend time in the sunshine and in the open air. Country folk are often more healthy than those of us who are imprisoned in concrete jungles, and this is one of the reasons why. Another is that natural power is absorbed by earth, trees, grass, flowers, etc., and radiated back. If we are able to walk in the country or in the park, walking on the grass if it is allowed, we can absorb some of these radiations. Leaning against a tree we absorb from the tree. Walking in a meadow full of buttercups, the very flowers that we crush with our feet offer up in their crushing a fragrance that is also a blessing. There is another link here with colour healing and with flower healing, both of which are being rediscovered in our time.

Higher Sources of Spiritual Power

While the foregoing gives a brief and sketchy outline of natural power, which normally keeps us healthy, and which, being natural and normal, is either unrecognized or taken for granted, it is obvious that we must look at power of a higher voltage so to speak, which is required to bring about healing where greater obstacles are in the way and have to be overcome.

This is where we may meet with some difficulty, for we have to conceive of a number of sources of great spiritual power and a number of readers may take exception to this. However my previous statement holds true. All power originates from God and we can call on that power. It matters not how we do this. When we begin a group healing session I usually make a silent prayer that goes something like this: 'Dear Lord, we ask that this room may be filled with thy light and thy power, that thy servants may use it to bring healing to those who come seeking help.'

As our knowledge of God is entirely subjective and very scanty, probably consisting of more doubts than certainties, many people in the Christian tradition would prefer to call upon Jesus. After all, Jesus is someone whom we can visualize – even if the origin of our mental picture is only from some dusty picture on a Sunday school wall. I presume that a lot of Christian ministers would say that it is not right to call upon anyone else for healing, quoting passages from the New Testament about 'asking in my name'. Some would argue that no other name should be used, that only by that name can healing come. With this I would not agree.

Great Spiritual Beings

Let us think of a number of Great Spiritual Beings, without physical bodies, but with 'bodies' of brilliant light, radiating that light, which is really love. These are those who, after much time, have grown near to God. Not physically near, as time and space are only worldly concepts. In their nearness, or in their 'likeness' to God, they too have become power-houses and transmitters of divine loving power. The Christ will be the greatest Great Spiritual Being for those within the Christian culture, but there will be others of equal eminence for those of other religions. Let us recognize that the divisions of faith and religion is also a thing of this world's making and while the followers of Moses, Krishna, Mohammed, Buddha or any other Teacher or Saviour may argue about the respective status of their own way, there is no enmity between the great names, for in the regions of light the law of harmony and unity reigns supreme.

Even within the Christian tradition there are others upon whose name we may call. There is Mary. There are the saints. Once again it is futile for us to argue about who is greater than whom. From our lowly position they are all far above us. They are all Great Spiritual Beings whose spirituality is such that all who call upon them can bask in the rays of the light and power that constantly radiate from them. (I use the word 'constantly' as a reminder that we must not think that something is 'switched-on' when we call.)

'Tuning In' to Spiritual Power

Think of it this way. Our ether is full of radio waves which carry countless radio signals from far away. While these signals are obviously sent out in the hope that they will be picked up, we hear nothing until, having a suitable instrument, *we* switch on and tune in. Then it is as if there was a direct link between our sitting-room and the station far away. This is largely illusory of course, another person hundreds of miles away can tune in to that same station without stealing our link or interfering with our reception. Indeed hundreds of thousands can tune in simultaneously.

We can apply this to our Great Spiritual Beings. If I say, 'I call upon the Christ that his power may be with us this evening', then I am switching on and tuning in to his wavelength, tapping radiations, and the power is there. And if I wish to visualize his face, his smile, his hands stretched out in blessing, then that is like turning up the volume. Should I feel moved to call upon the Great White Spirit, to tune in to another station so to speak, then the power will still be there, for all Good comes from the One Source.

While recognizing that my radio analogy is full of imperfections, let us stick with it for a little longer. The quality of reception largely depends on the quality of the instrument. In healing we are the instrument and, to put it simply, we must always be striving to make ourselves better receivers. It is also worth remembering that some radio receivers are never switched off, in the headquarters of the emergency services for example. Likewise those who seek to serve their fellows in healing should aim to be in a constant state of 'tuned-in-ness'.

We must, alas, embark upon another analogy before we leave our inadequate explanation of power. This time we think of electrical power. Of a great generating station, of other, lesser but still great, distribution centres. Of further channels, of transformers reducing the power until it is low enough, weak enough to enter into our houses. Even then it is too dangerous for us to touch, the power has to be dropped right down to a few volts before we could handle it without injury. Or perhaps it may be more useful to think of the power of the sun. If we got too close it would destroy us, whereas at our present distance of ninety-four million miles it is usually low enough to be of benefit to us. Usually but not always, as we all know from experiencing the discomfort of too much exposure to its summer holiday rays.

In a similar sort of way the power which brings healing begins as pure spirit, pure energy, and has to be stepped down, weakened, transformed, made in a sense coarser, before it can be transmitted to Auntie Maud who comes for healing, or before it can be channelled through the one who calls himself a healer. There is no way in which we can handle the mighty power unless it be so weakened. Having said that, it must also be said that the way is opening up. Spiritual evolution is happening and those who earnestly seek to develop spirituality within themselves will find that as they advance, so the power flowing through them will increase.

3

ARE HEALERS NECESSARY?

This is a question that has been asked many times. It is linked with another. 'Why aren't people automatically made well and kept well directly by God's spirit without the need for a go-between?' Another similar question which often puzzles sincere religious people concerns prayers for healing. If God knows that Auntie Maud is ill, why do we have to ask God to make her better? Can it be that he will not do anything unless and until we do ask? Have we to persuade God to be good? There is a deceptive simplicity about questions such as these, but there is nothing simple about the answers and for those who persist in thinking of God as a sort of superman, who lives somewhere up there and who can stretch forth his hands and touch our lives, for those there may not be any answer at all. However, there is a reasonable explanation as to why there needs to be a human element, a go-between if you like, in healing.

Planes of Existence

Every schoolboy these days learns that solid matter is not really solid at all but is simply a mass of atoms vibrating at certain frequencies and achieving a state of equilibrium or stability which makes it seem solid. Solid, that is, to anyone, or anything which is vibrating within the same frequency range. So we hurt ourselves when we stub our toe on a rock, even though we may know that, scientifically speaking, neither the rock nor our toe is really solid. Our painful experiment proves that stones and toes are vibrating within the same frequency range.

But suppose we were to see a ghost, a typical tourist attraction sort of ghost. It walks straight through the castle wall, through that offending rock and through us if we are standing in its path. Why? Because a ghost, using an etheric body, is vibrating at a higher or at least different rate. It may bump into another ghost in the same frequency range as itself, for its world is as solid to it as ours is to us. But ours is not solid to him and his is not solid to us. Are you still with me? It may be useful to recognize the seven planes of existence, that divide life into what, for simplicity, may be termed seven frequency ranges. At the top is the plane of pure spirit, while at the bottom is the material or physical plane. Let us say that the life vibrations are super-fine in the spiritual plane and ultra-coarse in the material. In theory there can be a gap, or at least a firm dividing line between one plane and the next. This is why our ghost cannot touch us, nor we it. In practice there is usually an over-lap and we live on more than one plane of existence. This overlapping makes for continuity and normally there is no reason why pure spirit should not reach us, subject to what was previously said about stepping-down or transforming the power. Normally we are constantly being bathed in the light of spirit, God if you prefer, and this produces and maintains health.

But if we do fall ill, the picture can change dramatically. We can withdraw into ourselves and this creates a definite gap between the physical plane and the higher planes. This is seen most frequently in mental depression.

Treatment of Depression

I am not a great lover of statistics but there seems no reason to doubt that mental depression is on the increase. There was a period when nearly all the visitors to our healing group were suffering from this most distressing condition. To the casual observer depression doesn't show and there is often little sympathy shown. 'Pull yourself together' is still said to one whose life is grey and weary and not worth living. Depression is one of the killer illnesses in that it often leads to suicide. As such it should never be taken lightly. Although it is usually called a mental illness, depression is more actually termed a spiritual illness. It was always recognized as such in times gone by when it was perhaps known as melancholia or accidie, and the priest was often seen as the person most likely to be of help.

It is true that only a fellow sufferer can understand the horrors of depression and the healer must always be particularly careful in his treatment of those who come to him for healing. It is also true that the sufferer from depression will not, at the beginning anyway, have much faith in spiritual healing, or much hope that the healer will be able to do anything. It is a last effort, a bottom of the barrel, 'well, it cannot do any more harm' attitude and quite often it is only the urging of a friend who says, 'I will come with you', that brings the depressed person to the healer's door.

Spiritually speaking, depression is caused by the coming into being, somehow or other, of a gap between the lowest and the higher planes of life. The spirit within, deprived of its spiritual nourishment from the higher planes, burns low and cold like a candle deprived of oxygen. As the colour and warmth fade from life, so does feelings for others. Faith goes, prayer is impossible, there is no God. The coldness and the withdrawal extends to family, including children, and this causes more distress.

I always stick my neck out with depression. I promise, I guarantee, that there will be an improvement. I stress that it will be a long hard slog but that in, say, six months the worst will be over. It is necessary to be bold in this way because we must create interest, we must kindle a spark of hope. Healing comes from within. By this I mean that that dimly burning wick of the divine spark, if nourished once again, will light up that life again.

The great problem with depression is getting the healing through, getting the divine power and love to the spirit within. Depression turns a person in on himself or herself and this creates a hard crust or shell that takes a lot of cracking, breaking and dispersing. This is what takes time, and there are very few short cuts.

It is this shell of course which breaks contact with God, which creates the gap between the higher vibrations and the lower. The answer is to use another human being, one who, although on the same level, within the same frequency range as the sufferer, is also in contact with higher frequencies. It is a case of down and then along. Down vertically and then along horizontally, rather like someone on the top floor of a block of flats wanting to contact someone on the ground floor. He contacts someone else on the ground floor who then goes along and delivers the message.

While depression is a rather special example of how and why human healers are used to do God's will, the principle outlined holds true in a general way and will be referred to and expanded later.

4

SPIRIT FRIENDS

We now come to one of the most important aspects of that activity known as spiritual healing. One that is, alas, difficult for many people to accept. It concerns the part that is played in the healing process by people who are no longer living on earth in flesh and blood bodies. In other words, spirits, or to use a phrase often used in theological discussion of the matter, discarnate entities. I dislike that phrase intensely and only mention it so that, should you ever come across it, you will understand that it means the same as 'spirits'.

Whatever the jargon, people who are in the world of spirit play an important part in healing. Many folk are reluctant to accept this, perhaps because of fear. They do not want to get mixed up in spiritualism or 'that sort of thing'. Perhaps the greatest opposition to the participation of spirit friends, or even to their very existence, comes from the ranks of orthodox Christians who recall Old Testament prohibitions on 'consulting the spirits' or who have been taught that the dead remain dead until the sounding of the last trump when all shall rise! We shall have more to say about this in the next chapter but we have to jump the gun a little here as we introduce the contribution of spirit friends in the work of a healer. The key to our understanding in this matter, as in so much else, is to let our common sense prevail. Whatever you have been taught in the past, whatever you have read, ask yourself, 'Does it make sense? Does it sound right?'

Judge this book in the same way. If in these pages you come across ideas that you have not come across before, do not dismiss them or accept them in a hurry. Weigh them carefully in your mind and use your common sense.

Now then, consider the case of a doctor who served the people of a town well. He could have made more money than he did. He could have had his brass plate in Harley Street, but he chose to remain in his working-class practice. His motive for doing so was quite simple. He cared for people.

The day came when he died. In his after-death state he elected to continue looking after his patients. (You should know that your personality does not change at death. You are still very much the same kind of person that you were on earth and what is more natural than such a man continuing to devote himself to the sick?) I did not know this particular doctor in the flesh, but on at least two occasions, when we have been giving healing to people who had been patients of his, he has been with us and has been seen standing in our healing room 'discussing the case' with one of our regular spirit healers. The latter is an Asian Indian who works with us and through us. He is our friend and part of our team.

Team Work

Healing is always a team exercise. There is no such thing as a healer working alone. Every one of us has a number of spirit helpers, whether we know it or not. Spiritualist healers, and here the capital 'S' is not just to begin the sentence but refers to healers who work within the Spiritualist movement, are glad to accept the reality of their 'spirit guides'. On the other hand, orthodox Christians, ministers or priests perhaps, are reluctant to do so, being eager to believe that all healing is of Christ. Some may go half-way, as it were, and recognize that there are 'ministering angels'. They need to be reassured that no one wants to deny the supreme significance of Christ. There may be problems with some of the doctrinal statements that have been made about Christ, but these problems exist within the Church as well as outside it. Nevertheless to very many people in the healing ranks, the Christ Light or the Spirit of Christ is the particular channel or wavelength that they seek to tune in to.

What is needed is a recognition of a sort of chain of lesser beings tapping into the power supply. Whether one speaks of angels and archangels, whether one prefers to recognize the saints, or whether one thinks of good people of all centuries, saintly perhaps, but not saints, doesn't really matter. But it is perfectly reasonable to me to accept that if I, as a very unsaintly flesh and blood person, can tap the source of divine power for service to my fellows, then so can those who are no longer companions of the flesh. Indeed it is easier for those in spirit, for God is spirit and the power is also spirit. In theory there is no reason why I, when I die, should not continue my healing work, this time from the other side of the fence, perhaps working with another earthly minister of a younger generation.

Spirit Guides

I would not wish to be slow in praising the great achievements gained by the Spiritualist movement in Great Britain, particularly in healing and in teaching; but it must be admitted that there are two faces to spiritualism. There is, for example, a kind of snobbery concerning 'spirit guides' and we are all familiar with the Red Indian, the Chinese and the Egyptian guides. At the last spiritualist service I was at, the guest speaker had an interesting point to make concerning this. 'You treat them as second-class citizens when they are in your world,' she said, 'but you are proud to have them as your guides when they have passed over.' I also remember a petulant letter to the editor of a Spiritualist newspaper. The writer said that he had always understood that his guide was a certain Red Indian chief, but he had recently been talking to another chap who said that that chief was *his* guide, how can this be? Am I being unfair in thinking that those two had been almost bragging about their spiritual connections? Name dropping with a new twist!

The editor, who I suspect is sick and tired of that sort of thing, dealt beautifully with his reader's query: 'With so many Chiefs about, whatever happened to all the Indians?'

Of course there are a lot of spirit friends who have been members of those highly evolved races. I am talking now, of course, of spiritual evolution, not technological. The proof of their spiritual progress lies in the very numbers who are still serving mankind. For the most part they do it anonymously, unseen and unnoticed. In established healing groups some of them may let their presence be known, but this is for our benefit, not theirs, and it only happens at our request. That is why those who do not believe in such people are not likely to have reason to change their minds! We certainly find that being conscious of the unseen members of our team is a great help to us, although we only know about half a dozen of them. One of our unknowns sent us a brief message of introduction: 'I come from a land of beauty, sunshine and music, my heart is sore at the atrocities of my people.' What a sad commentary on our 'advanced' but war-torn world.

The service of these spirit friends is truly one of love and the words of the old prayer come to mind.

Teach us, good Lord, to serve thee as thou deservest,
To give and not to count the cost,
To fight and not to heed the wounds,
To labour and not to ask for any reward
Save that of knowing that we do thy will.

There are of course many spirit helpers who are of our own race. The time of spiritual darkness that gripped this country for so long is passing and many more are following the path of spiritual development. It is heart-warming that the good doctor referred to earlier should wish to continue his healing service, and there are many like him. It must also be said that the spirit side of a long-established healing group is quite likely to contain members who were previously active on the physical side and who, at death, simply changed their position in the team.

5

'THERE IS NO DEATH!'

It is another sad commentary on our times that, although the so-called facts of life are taught to all our children and, in theory, are known by everyone, the facts of death do not get a mention. The consequence of this is that there is a great ignorance concerning the end of this physical life. Ignorance is a good breeding ground for fear and so many of our contemporaries are afraid of dying.

Fear of Cancer

There are many unfortunate spin-offs from this. The one that bothers me most is the conspiracy of silence that surrounds terminal illness, particularly cancer. There is a familiar pattern that I have come across many times in my ministry. Bill Smith, for want of a better name, one of my parishioners, lies in hospital. The cancer is inoperable and the doctors have a quiet word with the family. So often in these cases it is decided that Bill should not be told and so a gulf is created between him and his family at the very time when they should be close together. How much better was the case of M., a lady member of one of our groups. An earlier bout of cancer had been beaten back, giving her another five years of service, but this time it was terminal. The family discussed it with her and she decided to discharge herself from hospital, preferring to die in her own bed.

The following evening I was sent for as her time was near. When I went into the room she was whispering non-stop, incoherently, I must admit, but I caught enough to realize that she was still trying to help others. I put my hands on her and said, 'Come on M., enough is enough; your friends are waiting for you and it's time to go.' She gently slipped away under my touch. I went downstairs and told the family that she had gone. 'That's good', they said. There was no weeping or wailing. They knew where she was and whom she was with, there was no need for tears. Needless to say, fear of dying is a great obstacle to healing. Fear of any sort is an enemy of the spirit. It sets up a kind of 'force-field' of grey vibrations that blocks the healing rays.

It is said that 'Perfect faith casts out fear'. That is probably quite true but how many have perfect faith? Laughter is a simpler alternative. Certainly it can help to solve the healing problem for the vibrations of laughter break up and disperse the grey force-field of fear. Unless the fear itself is removed, however, the grey mesh can re-form.

As fear is caused by ignorance then let our object be to impart knowledge and information, making known the unknown. Let us deal in facts, and the most important fact at this juncture is the blunt heading to this chapter. There is no death. What we are really talking about is life, or rather about two kinds of life.

Material Life and Spiritual Life

By material life I mean this body of flesh and blood, bone and sinew. As the Bible and the Burial Service remind us it is created from dust and to dust it shall return. In other words my body is part and parcel of this planet Earth. As such it shares in the wonderful economy and harmony of Earth where nothing is ever wasted, but nothing is ever static. Things grow and decay in a harmonious cyclic movement. Trees grow, taking nourishment from the soil. When they fall and decay they feed the soil on which they lie so that other trees might grow. The cyclic movement may be described as upward, around, and down. Our body, being earthy, follows this pattern. Up, as we grow, then over the peak and down. Earth to earth, ashes to ashes, dust to dust. We can predict the lifespan of earthly things. Some insects only live a few hours. Trees follow their species, oaks spending more time on the cyclic round than conifers. The cycle of the human body has, in Biblical terms, a seventy year run, three score years and ten, from its rising to its falling.

Now we turn to spiritual life and once again there is a cyclic pattern, but this time the direction is the other way round. The divine spark, the spirit which is the *real* me, proceeds from God downwards and then returns on an upward course. In other words there is a fall, from God, followed by a climb towards God. The time taken to complete this cycle cannot really be measured by our standards of time but it is certainly in the thousands of years!

Does this surprise you? It ought not to. It ought to be something that you were made conscious of at your mother's knee – Although it is just possible that at that time you knew more about life than your mother did. There is a strong theory that an infant has knowledge of what has gone before, knowledge which is quickly overlaid as it proceeds to learn the ways of its new environment. Some friends of ours had an interesting experience of this. They had been talking about death when their three-year-old chipped in, 'When you die not all of you dies, God keeps a bit and uses it again'.

Out of the mouths of babes and sucklings . . .

So, the real me is spirit, and I am on a journey. On this journey I gather up experience and wisdom, I grow in spiritual stature. My aim is to complete the journey and to return to my home base. The spirit me desires union with God. God is spirit – deep calls unto deep and 'Our souls are restless until they find their rest in thee'.

Reincarnation

At this stage in our evolution we are experiencing life on earth. Learning the lessons that life here can teach us, transmuting this knowledge into spiritual wisdom that will take us another step nearer God.

How long it takes depends to some extent on our knowing what we have to do and getting on with it, but it takes much longer than the cyclic life on earth will allow at one go. In other words we have to live on earth a number of times, and each time we come we have to build around ourselves a material body which only lasts, on average, something like the biblical three score and ten years. This is called reincarnation, a concept that is currently out of favour in our Western world where the presumption is that we only live on earth once. Once again we are called upon to use our common sense. The once only theory leads us to think that life is full of inequalities – and many people to blame God for the unfairness of life. Let us look at a few examples.

A life of abject poverty. Particularly when it is a good person who is poor while all around the rotters seem to prosper.

With reincarnation in mind we can suggest reasons for a life of poverty. Certainly a full experience of life would include the experience of being poor and hungry. There is much to learn from such an experience. It is a test that will demand great fortitude from us and if we win through, the soul will be greatly strengthened. But I mentioned abject poverty, and it may be that the severity of the experience arises from the faulty handling of a previous experience. Perhaps in the last life we were rich and did not learn the great lessons that wealth can teach us. One can well imagine that Marie Antoinette ('Let them eat cake') may well have been born a poor peasant girl next time round.

Or consider an 'untimely death'. How do we react when a child or young person dies? Do we say it is tragic? A terrible waste? Do we say, 'How can a God of love allow such a thing to happen?' Certainly an untimely death is frustrating, but only in the sense that time has been lost. It can best be seen as similar to a schoolboy who, injured in a football match, has to miss his exams and must wait until next term.

Indeed the whole business of reincarnation can be likened to going to a boarding school. Life on earth is the boarding school. At the end of each term we go home for a break, when we assimilate and evaluate what we have learned. During this time we work out what our next set of lessons should be, what courses we need to retake, what new courses, tests, experiences, we are ready for and so the pattern of our next life is laid down. The tricky problem is that when we are reborn, quite apart from the necessity of going through infancy, childhood, etc., all over again, we have no conscious memory of what we are supposed to do or what we have done before. There are exceptions to this of course. If we can realize the truth about life, that we are spirit, and that this material round is but one episode, then we can develop spiritual insight into the purpose of this particular incarnation and, perhaps, recover some memories from past episodes. This in fact happens more often than people realize, but so often these memories are not recognized for what they are.

A friend of mine recently moved into a flat in an old house and was told, psychically, that she had lived in that house in a previous life. I asked one of our spirit friends if it would help her to know the circumstances of that past life, and was told bluntly, 'No!' This seems to indicate that it is not always wise to press for prior-life memories. They may do more harm than good.

There was a time when belief in reincarnation was part of the Christian teachings, but it was dropped, more's the pity, and today Christianity is the only great religion that cannot offer its followers a balanced teaching on life. There is a story from Scotland which illustrates this. After a funeral the widow asked the minister if there *was* an after-life. 'We can but hope,' he replied. 'Hope be damned, man, you're paid to know.' How true, how very true.

I would urge the reader whose mind baulks at reincarnation, to pursue the subject. Any public library will have enough books to get him started, while some of those mentioned at the end of this book will also help.

A last point concerns the strange phenomena of child prodigies, children whose musical or mathematical prowess is out of all proportion to their tender years. It seems to me that the most reasonable explanation for this is that they are in some way linking two lives together, carrying on almost where the last one left off. Arrangements seem to have been made for them to be born into families who are willing and able to foster their abilities.

There is no point in going any deeper into reincarnation in a book which aims to concentrate on healing. What we are trying to establish at the moment is that *this* life, in *this* body, while it is important, is not *all-*important.

We know that we are in this body for a limited time and will some day have to leave it. Let us not be afraid of that day or that leaving.

Think of it as a man using a motor car for his travels. He looks after his car; he has it repaired when something goes wrong, he may grow quite fond of it and hope to have it for a long time. He may be unfortunate and have an accident whereby the car is, as they say, 'written off'. Even so, the time will come when fair wear and tear takes its toll and it has to go to the scrap yard. There the man leaves it and eventually takes another car. We leave our bodies when they 'die', but we do not die with them. It is the journey that is important, not the vehicle. Although we have a duty to our vehicle, our body, to look after it, we should not fear its demise.

Some spiritually evolved people know when their body will die, and they know this well in advance of the time. This gives gives them the opportunity to complete their tasks and to tie up the loose ends, put their affairs in order and so on. This knowledge is hidden from the majority of us because we are not able to cope with it. I suppose that is why Bill Smith's doctors are reluctant to tell him that his time is near. Incidentally it is not only doctors who are faced with this problem of 'to tell or not to tell'. Clairvoyants, even fortune-tellers, often see death. My African witch-doctor friend had terrible problems with regard to this. He was a natural seer and his premonitions of death were always accurate. He would never tell the person concerned, mainly because he could never think of a safe way of doing so, but he told me of trying to persuade a friend not to go to London by car but to take a train. He was not persuasive enough and he knew as his friend drove away that there would be an accident and his friend would be killed. He once attended an interview for a job and was dismayed to see that the personnel officer interviewing him only had about six weeks to live. As he said afterwards, 'How could I, an African, tell him that. He would have called the cops and accused me of cursing him.'

This psychic ability was a terrible burden to my friend. Many people these days seem to be eager to develop psychic gifts. They perhaps do not realize that they will see and experience the bad as well as the good.

6

WHAT IS HEALING?

The concept of yourself, the real you, as spirit, is one that must be firmly grasped before you can develop an understanding of healing. It is a foundation stone upon which the understanding will be built.

When I speak of healing I mean spiritual healing. You may have heard other terms and wondered if there were differences between faith healing, divine healing, spirit healing and spiritual healing.

Newspapers seem to prefer the term, faith healing. To me this is a woefully inadequate term. It suggests that there is no need to *know*. I am all for learning of the hows and the whys and the wherefores. Faith is probably a useful thing, although if it is based on misconceptions it can be a nuisance. It is better if knowledge is added to faith. Like everything else in this universe, healing is subject to natural laws and we should seek to understand these laws.

Divine healing is a churchy phrase, probably only used to emphasize that God is the source of healing power.

Spirit healing? I think I am right in saying that this is used as a reminder of the part played by spirit friends in the healing process. It does not contradict the previous emphasis, that the power is really from a divine source, but it is a useful reminder to the human healer that he is not as clever as he is sometimes tempted to think he is. A bit of ego-bashing is necessary every now and then, particularly in the early months. A healer must remember that he is only a channel, a medium, a pipeline.

Spiritual healing can have two meanings, in theory if not in practice. It can mean the healing that is offered at Spiritualist Churches. There is a

National Federation of Spiritual Healers, founded by Harry Edwards, and so spiritual healing has become a sort of technical term, perhaps even with exclusive overtones.

It is in the second sense of the phrase that I use it, namely that spiritual healing is healing of the spirit by the spirit. This, of course, is not usually appreciated by those who come for healing. Mrs Smith with her arthritis, and Miss Smith with colitis, are only concerned with getting rid of pain and discomfort and may wonder why the healer puts his hands on their heads, when the trouble is obviously, to them, somewhere else. As I usually do begin healing by resting my hands lightly on the head, I find it useful to explain that this is to help the person to relax. This is actually very important for tension acts as a barrier to the healing rays and both the recipient and the healer must be relaxed to facilitate an easy passage. There are other reasons why the head is a good place to start. Two of the major psychic centres of the body, chakras in Eastern teaching, are situated in the head so this is an obvious starting point. Furthermore it is quite common for someone who is ill, or even nervous at coming to a healer, to have a headache, and as these are easily got rid of, why not do that first?

I have forgotten how troublesome headaches can be, although there was a time when I always kept aspirin handy for headaches, even though I probably had no more headaches than anyone else. Nowadays if I get so much as a twinge I tell it to go away, and it does, immediately.

A Simple Healing Technique

I have often advised people who are wondering if they can do healing to practise on someone's headache. Perhaps you would like to try. Let us suppose that someone in your family has come home with a 'splitting' headache. Before they reach for the pills, ask them if you can try and give them a bit of healing. If they agree, sit them in a chair, an ordinary hard-backed chair will do, and ask them to try to relax, possibly by taking a few deep breaths. Stand behind them and do the same to get yourself relaxed. Offer up a silent prayer: 'Use me, dear Lord, as a channel for thy healing spirit, that this headache may be dispersed.'

Put your hands gently on the head (never be a heavy-handed healer). An alternative stance is slightly to one side of the chair so that you can put one hand on the forehead and the other at the nape of the neck. Continue to relax and do not worry about failing or making a fool of yourself. After a minute or so, begin to use your imagination. Imagine that the the pain is being drawn to your hands, leaving the head and entering your hands. Lift your hands off and the pain comes away. Shake your hands or flick your fingers to get rid of it. Or you can imagine that you are actually seeing the headache, perhaps like grey cobwebs covering the head. Scoop it all up gently and throw it away. This will have taken, say, three minutes. Remove your hands and ask if anything has happened. The recipient will probably answer in a surprised voice, 'Well, it seems to have eased', but will probably add that it is still bad around the area of the temples. Repeat the process, concentrating on these areas. You can also try telling the headache to go away. I will explain this later in the book.

The end result of all this will be that you either have or have not removed the headache. If it has gone you will be greatly encouraged and you will begin to think seriously of offering yourself for healing. If it hasn't gone you will naturally be disappointed. But think about the episode for a minute. You have been trying to do something which a short time ago you might have classed as a miracle. Are you really surprised that it didn't all come right first time? Were either you or your guinea pig creating some sort of barrier, consciously or unconsciously? It is worth asking whether your hands felt hotter or perhaps colder than normal. This is often a sign that the healing power is there.

7

THE ETHERIC BODY

This is where we introduce one of those concepts that you may not have come across before, something about which you may have reservations or even doubts. But I do urge you, if only to preserve the unity of the book, to carefully assimilate this section on the etheric body. It will illuminate a number of points which have already been mentioned, but not fully explained, and it will also be a useful point of reference.

The etheric body is most simply understood as a duplicate of the physical body. For this reason it is often called the etheric 'double'. Imagine that you are wearing a close-fitting skin suit of fine mesh, following every contour of your body.

What is it made of? The etheric body is really a system of electromagnetic stresses. It is energy. The remarkable series of photographs taken by the Kirlians, showing a glow radiating from the edges of living things and often thought to be photographs of the aura, are probably showing the edges of the etheric counterparts to the physical objects.

The etheric body grows with you and remains inseparably part of you until your body dies. Then the etheric body leaves and can sometimes be seen by psychics. The etheric body is said to be the vehicle of the spirit, for it vibrates at the same frequency of the spirit. The etheric body is more than just a skin suit, it is not just a covering: it permeates the whole of the physical body. Every part of the physical body has its etheric counterpart. This accounts for the extraordinary difference between a live body and a dead body. Not only to the senses of touch, sight and smell but in many indefinable ways, a dead body is different. The etheric has left, the life has left.

An old body, dying properly and gently, often dies 'from the feet up'. The feet become cold and lifeless, then the legs, etc. This can be distressing to see or feel if one does not know what is going on, but if one had psychic vision one would see the etheric body slowly separating from the physical, 'from the feet up'.

Not only does the etheric permeate the physical body, it also feeds it. Not with material sustenance, food and drink, but with the energies of life, the spiritual energies. Thus when we said that in colour healing the filtered rays were absorbed, this is how it happens. They are absorbed by the 'energy field' that is the etheric body.

When we wrote of absorbing natural power from sun, earth, trees, flowers, etc., this power is also absorbed as rays of energy by the etheric body.

When I spoke of someone being surrounded by beautiful amethyst rays, it was the etheric that was being re-charged.

It is the etheric, spiritual, body that is involved when we give healing. That is why healing works. The spiritual side of life, and this includes what I loosely call spiritual power, and also those whom I call spirit friends, has a direct link with your etheric body.

Because the etheric permeates and in one sense duplicates the physical body, sickness of the physical is reflected in its etheric counterpart. Hence by healing the etheric we also heal the physical, for the health of the etheric is reflected in the physical.

Minor irritations, such as might cause a headache, are largely irritations of the etheric which are reflected upon the physical, possibly upon the central nervous system. So when you put your hands upon your relative's head, and when you drew the headache into your hands, you were drawing away from his or her etheric, into yours, by a simple process of magnetic attraction. And when you visualized the headache 'like cobwebs' and scooped it up and threw it away, you were ridding him or her of contaminated etheric matter.

Once again I am in danger of over-simplification, but at least you now understand, or I hope you do, what I meant when I said that healing was a natural process, following natural laws. Perhaps you also understand my previous statement that anyone can give healing, if he wishes, and that the belief that healing is a special kind of holy gift, is erroneous.

Let us now go back to the beginning and ask ourselves the question: 'What is a Healer?' A healer is a person who cares for people. Someone who has a deep compassion and an earnest desire to help his fellow men and fellow women.

He is religious in the sense that he believes that God is good. He is one who, in his earnest desire to help, offers his services, nay, offers his life, as a channel, as a medium, through which healing may be given to those who are in need of it.

He will seek to strengthen his links with God. By prayer and meditation he will seek his own spiritual development – but not for his own sake. His motive in seeking the highest will be unselfish. In humility he will realize that he is indeed an imperfect vessel.

8

THE AURA

Just as every person has an etheric body so does he or she have an aura. The two are connected but they are not the same. The spiritual aura, as I prefer to call it, has been described as a magnetic field of vibration which surrounds a person, just as light surrounds a candle or perfume surrounds a flower. The aura radiates in all directions to a distance varying from a few inches to a few feet.

As far as healing is concerned there are four important points to make regarding the aura.

(1) *Disease shows in the aura.* There are a large number of people who can see the aura, though I confess that I am not one of them. Some years ago a certain Dr Kilner invented a screen through which people with ordinary vision could view auras. Since then a number of doctors have carried out experiments with 'Kilner screens'. The tentative conclusions reached tend to support the claims made by people with 'psychic' vision that disease shows in the aura, usually as a shadow or darker patch. This shadow appears in the very early stages of the condition. Obviously this is a very useful form of early diagnosis and one hopes that research will continue. It promises to be a very fruitful field of enquiry.

(2) *Healing rays are absorbed by the aura.* As with the etheric body, the aura is essentially something which is vibrating at frequencies higher than that of the physical body. These may be easiest explained as vibrations of light, for the aura is really a complex of colours, delicate, iridescent, soft. When a healer is touching someone, his own aura is often being charged with the correct type of ray, in the appropriate amount and intensity, and

this he is passing on. Often one of the spirit helpers is doing this charging, directing the rays into the healer's aura.

(3) *The character of a person is shown by the colours, the size and the intensity of his aura.* Hence one's aura reveals exactly the virtues and vices that go to make up one's personality and character. People who are compassionate, loving and unselfish would have large bright auras, while selfishness leads to a contraction of the aura and a darkening of the colours.

When I was talking about people who suffer from depression I mentioned a sort of hard shell around them which acted as a barrier to the healing rays. As it is normal for a depressive to turn in on himself, and to have little feelings for others, which is a form of selfishness really, it is the tight dark aura which acts as the barrier. Saintly people often have golden hues in their auras and this is the origin of haloes in religious paintings, although it must be said that the saints of this world are more likely to be those who battle against heavy odds in life, in deprived circumstances perhaps, rather than ecclesiastics in the cloisters.

As the aura is a true reflection of our personality it can often give the lie to the kind of person we think we are or would have others think. In any case, when we leave the body the truth about us remains and in spirit that truth stands revealed. If we would only realize that our true selves are on open display, as it were, to those who have the eyes to see, then perhaps we would be more serious in our efforts to make ourselves better people.

It is said that clergymen have certain distinctive hues in their aura. My Anglican friend at Bellingham once told me a lovely story about a little old lady in Wales. One Sunday at church they had a guest preacher, an Australian who was appealing on behalf of some obscure aboriginal mission. After the service she buttonholed the regular parson and whispered, 'That man is not a real priest'. She was so adamant that the Bishop was informed and discreet enquiries were made. It turned out that the Australian had once undergone some theological training but had been dismissed for dishonesty and had subsequently developed a new line in confidence trickery.

When the little old lady was asked what had made her suspicious she answered simply, 'He didn't have the light!' She may or may not have known what an aura was but she knew that a glow emanated from her 'proper' priest and it hadn't from the bogus one.

I was reminded of this story a few months ago when I was wandering around our local shopping precinct. I was not wearing my clerical collar, in fact I was wearing something from an army surplus store. Once again it was a little old lady who, as she passed, smiled at me and said, 'God bless you, Father'. The concluding section of the last chapter, when we asked 'What is a Healer?', was to remind you, and perhaps to remind myself as well, that a healer must set himself the highest standard. In reaching up, his character will change, and this will show in his 'light'.

(4) *Auras can merge into one another.* This contact between auras is of great importance, in two ways. The aura of a healer expands as he develops, and grows really large when he is actually healing, perhaps to three to four feet in all directions. This means that as he stands close to someone he is almost enveloping them in his light. The term 'laying-on of hands' is often used as synonymous with 'contact healing', but in practice many healers may not touch the other person at all but simply hold their hands a few inches away from the other's body. The auras are in contact, the healing rays are passing from one to the other, and that will be sufficient.

On the other hand auric contact can work in the other direction and you may pick up vibrations that you could well do without. This is particularly so in the early stages of development when the aura is growing and opening. The next time you go into a crowded store, just have a look at the people there. See the many drawn, frowning, unsmiling faces. Unhappy faces, faces that show tension and sadness. You walk among them, with an aura that is in a tender stage of growth and suddenly you've got a headache, or you are feeling dizzy, sick or faint. One of the first things you must learn is how to seal the aura. We sometimes call this putting the barriers up or wrapping oneself up. This involves mind pictures, a very important activity with many applications in healing. Picture a barrier around yourself. The kind of barrier you erect in thought is largely a matter of choice. I used to visualize myself encased in a wall of steel shutters, another of our members would picture herself as being totally enclosed within a protective bubble. Whichever way it is done the primary thought is that you are sealing yourself off from all those bad vibrations. You are protecting yourself. If you do not do this then you are asking for trouble.

9

CONTACT HEALING: THE GROUP

It is now time for me to explain what happens in a healing group. Perhaps I ought to have added a chapter on 'How to get Started in Healing', but let us presume that you have made contact with a group that meets regularly for healing and that you have received an invitation to sit in on one of their meetings. Your first problem, or rather my first problem, is that there is no such thing as a typical healing group. There are so many different ways of going about things that all I can do is to go through the sort of things that happen at our healing group, leaving you to remember that any group that you are invited to may be totally different.

A Typical Healing Meeting
So let us suppose that you are coming to one of our meetings, what happens? Well, first of all we meet in a room in my house. Ideally a healing room should not be used for anything else. In practice it is likely to be the sitting-room or lounge which is normally used by the family and is likely to be contaminated by any frustrations, tempers, tensions or problems that have bothered the family that day. These all leave bad vibrations in the atmosphere of the room. So the room must be cleared. Physical cleaning might include vacuuming, dusting and a general tidying up. If possible this should be done well beforehand and the room left for an hour or so. During this time some of our spirit friends will come and do some psychic cleaning, getting rid of those bad vibrations.

As we get near the appointed hour the members of the group arrive and there is a chorus of greetings and general chatter. Then we settle down. We need to start tuning in. Perhaps we play a record, mood music I suppose you could call it. Some groups sing a hymn and follow with a prayer. We light a candle and this will burn throughout the meeting. When we are settling down we can look at the candle and use it to focus our thoughts on light and warmth and love, the Light of the World perhaps. We are thinking of why we are here. As we do this we are perhaps breathing deeply, both to relax and to fill ourselves with light. When this is happening our auras are expanding, perhaps merging with each other, but certainly growing and glowing. We are going to be both receivers, and givers of power.

Because we are still in need of protection against the dark shadows, I seal the room. I put mental barriers up around the whole room, probably around the house as well. I say my little silent prayer, 'Dear Lord, let this room be filled with thy light and thy healing power, that we might serve those who come for help.' Some of our spirit friends will be with us, those whose task it is to channel the light and power, those who have knowledge in healing, those who are standing guard. Others will be already accompanying those people who will be coming for healing this evening, perhaps conversing with the spirits who normally watch over them. For none is alone, each one of us has someone close in spirit.

A knock at the door. Our first visitor arrives. A lady who has an internal complaint and who is shortly to go into hospital for a major operation. Our healing task here is two-fold. We will give her healing for the complaint itself but we will also aim to give her strength and a more tranquil frame of mind than she has at the moment, for she is a little apprehensive about the operation. She has been to us before and we have told her what we are doing and she is already less frightened than she was when she first came.

After some general chatter I put a chair into the middle of the semi-circle; we like to sit in a semi-circle if we can. She sits on the chair and makes herself comfortable. I ask her to relax and to look at the candle if she wishes to do so.

I stand behind her and place my hands on her shoulders. This helps her to relax and I feel the tension gradually easing away from her. Then I move my hands to her head and become conscious of my breathing. As I breathe in I imagine that I am breathing in light and power, as I breathe out I see this being poured into her. The rest of the group are sitting quietly, probably with their eyes closed and their hands either cupped one in the other, or held with the palms facing towards the lady in the chair.

I may or may not receive a thought message from one of the spirit healers to move my hands. For example, I may feel that I want to place one hand in the small of her back. In all likelihood she will say, 'Oh, that's nice. How did you know that my back has been troubling me all day?'

In any case, after about five minutes I begin to wind up. I make slow stroking movements, across her shoulders then down her arms, hands and fingers. I am actually getting rid of waste etheric matter. The effect of the healing treatment is as good as a tonic and the lady feels very refreshed. When she leaves the chair to go and sit on the settee, I brush the chair down as well, with my hand, and then go into the kitchen and wash my hands – all to do with getting rid of waste matter that has been drawn out or forced out by the in-going healing power. We all 'take five', and the second visitor arrives. Actually there are two of them, a lady with 'nerves' and a friend who has come along to give moral support. This is a first visit for them. Their only previous contact with me has been via the telephone. 'Someone gave me your name and I wondered . . .'

We have arranged the timetable so that they arrive while the first lady is still here. We know from experience that the presence of someone else who is on the receiving end, as it were, can be a great help to a first timer.

So it is in this instance, and the first lady is very sympathetic and reassuring. When she leaves, after another ten minutes or so, the newcomers are beginning to relax. We chat and I ask questions about the 'nerves'. It is our old enemy depression again, accompanied by a constant tremor of the arms as if she was permanently shivering with cold. Perhaps she is.

When she is in the chair she feels a lot of heat from my hands. I am not conscious of this heat and in fact my hands are not hot, but they are to her. This is a well-known phenomenon in healing. A few months ago I was on the receiving end and as one of the group put her hands on my back her hands seemed to be burning holes right through me. It was not painful or in any way distressing (healing power never does any harm), but the heat was intense. The person who was giving me that healing is usually conscious of this heat in her hands whereas I never am. There is so much variation in healing, due to a large extent to the activity of our spirit friends, who are always active, although the 'sensitivity' of the healer is also a factor.

We spend a long time with this lady with the nervous depression. The tremors cease while she is in the chair but start up again when she goes back to the settee. As I have said before, depression is a long hard slog.

Our third visitor is also a depressive, and I am glad that the others have gone before she arrives for she is very down in the dumps. She has had a terrible week.

I slowly tell her again of things that I have said before. I remind her that when she first started coming to us, each day of every week was a black day. Then one week she had a good day. After a few weeks she was having two or three good days. I had pointed out to her that when she reached the stage of having four good days in a week, then that week would have been more good than bad.

On this occasion I have to remind her that healing for depression is often a case of two steps forward and one step back. I remind her of the tide coming in on the sea-shore. It comes forward, then it slips back apparently defeated. But this slipping back is also a gathering of strength for the next coming forward, and this time it travels a little further. Eventually after much coming and going, it gets to where it wants to be. There are times when we all need reminding of the rhythms of life, of the ebb and flow of the life-forces, and I find this illustration of the tide to be particularly useful.

This third lady is our last visitor for the evening and when she goes we relax. It has been hard work and for a little while we are tired. But we soon brighten up again. Anyway we are not finished yet for we have some absent healing to do. One of our members sets up about a dozen photographs. These are of people who have written in for healing and we have written back asking for a photograph. Very useful things, photographs. I do not quite know why but a photograph always has something of the subject in it. This makes it a useful link. It also gives us a face that we can picture, which is also very useful, particularly as most people try to look happy when they are being photographed and this is exactly how we want to see them.

We are an undisciplined lot in our group and even though the photographs are up we are still chatting. The lady who looks after the photographs tells us of a few telephone calls from some of those people, reporting progress, all of it good this week. While all this is going on, another member, who happens to be very psychic, sees one of our spirit healers standing in front of the photographs with his hands raised in blessing. As she mentions this we come to order and settle down, concentrating on each of the faces in turn and sending healing. For this was the purpose of A., our spirit friend, letting himself be seen. To remind us, in a very gentle way, to get on with it! The psychic member not only saw A., she 'heard' the prayer he was 'speaking' and afterwards wrote it down. This is it.

In the name of God the Father and the Holy Ghost,
may the healing water flow around you evermore and
envelope each aching body I see before me, and I ask
God's help to pass through my hands the healing
stream around each one.

Our session is now drawing to a close. We should end with a prayer of thanksgiving, but we are not as formal about this as perhaps other groups are. Nevertheless, we are thankful and grateful for the privilege of being in the healing group. We make a pot of tea and there is much to talk about. Impressions received when the healing was going on, our thoughts on this visitor and that visitor. New ideas that we might try next time. Every meeting is different. There is always something new. More often than not things do not go exactly as we planned them beforehand, but it is always wonderful. We perhaps forget to seal our auras before we leave but our spirit friends seem to take care of that for us.

And when we have gone, some of the unknown spirit friends, refuse collectors you might say, come and remove from the room all the waste etheric matter, all the vibrations of sadness and depression, and the room is returned for family use tomorrow.

While this description is of one particular healing group at work, it should be understood that there are no hard and fast rules regarding the procedure to be followed. A lot depends on where a group meets.

If healing sessions are held in a church, either within the sanctuary itself or in a vestry, then the surroundings will bring some influence to bear on the way the meeting is organized and run. One of the great disadvantages of the meeting I have described is that we only have the use of one room. It can often be a great help to have two rooms, a waiting room and a healing room. We have to rely on a timetable and hope that people will not come before or after their agreed time. This often goes wrong, and on occasions we have had the room full of people. This is best avoided if at all possible.

Obviously the leader of a group tends to influence the group. A parson may well wish to conduct the actual healing in the form of a service, with hymns and prayers, and with people coming forward one at a time for healing as they might come forward for the sacramental bread and wine at the Eucharist. A third influential factor lies in the parent group. A lot of groups grow out of other groups and may want to do things in the same way. On the other hand they may want to do things differently. In either case the methods used in the parent group will have been taken into account.

Methods, procedures, rituals, these things are really unimportant. What really matters is that all the members are content with the system and feel relaxed. In any case there will always be changes and adaptations as the group grows into a team and evolves into an effective healing force. Better ways of doing things will suggest themselves from time to time. Changes of personnel will also occur, someone drops out, someone else is invited to join in, the group may get too big and divide into two, all these things can happen. With each change, the dynamics of the group will change and the 'older' members must be flexible enough to adapt to the new situation.

Avoidance of Negative Attitudes

If something goes wrong within the group, resulting from a clash of personalities perhaps, then the leader has a problem. He must be strong enough to have the matter brought out into the open. Any sense of grievance, resentment or any other negative attitude will severely hamper the healing and must be talked out. Members of a healing group draw very close to each other and as the relationship deepens, differences may show that were not apparent on the surface. It sometimes happens that the only sensible thing to do is to suspend operations for a while and in severe cases of discord it may be better to disband the group altogether.

It will be appreciated that the composition of a group is of great importance. Members must be *en rapport* with each other. Often a group is largely composed of members of the same family.

Looking for a Group

Earlier on I suggested that if you were interested in healing it might be useful to find a group and ask to sit in. If you do this, be prepared for a searching examination by the leader regarding your reasons and motives. Be prepared for a refusal. It may be that you would not fit in to that group. It may be that they have recently had a change of personnel and need to settle down again before opening their ranks to another newcomer, even an observer. It may be that the ideas taught in this book, which will to some extent have become your ideas, will be totally unacceptable to the group you have approached. There may be many reasons why your initial approach to a healing group may prove abortive. It might simply be a case of hunting around until you find one that suits you. Or you could seek to start a group among your own family and friends. Of one thing you can be sure. If you want to do healing, a way will be found. Your spirit friends will see to that.

It may be that in describing the activities of an established healing group I have started at the wrong end of the healing scene. There are other, simpler healing endeavours which may be more suitable for beginners and these will be dealt with in due course.

'Dark Shadows'

Before I do that I must refer back to that description of a meeting of our group and explain about 'dark shadows'.

The phrase arose, you may remember, in the context of explaining the sealing or protecting of the healing room. Filling the place with light and not giving hospitality to 'dark shadows'.

By these I mean spirits that may cause harm or mischief. Our parent group always referred to them as entities, so we do the same, but it may be that you have come across the terms, 'lost souls', or 'earth-bound spirits'. The explanation of these simple terms, which mean roughly the same thing, is far from simple, but enough has already been said to enable me to introduce that explanation at this point.

When someone dies a natural death, gently and peacefully, he (or she) will gradually lose consciousness of this world and become conscious of the spirit world. This may be spread over a period of days or even weeks. On the spirit side there is an awareness that death is near, although they prefer to think of it as birth, birth into a new dimension, and preparations are made, just as we might prepare for the birth of a new baby. Part of these preparations is the gathering of friends and relations who assist in the transition. The 'dying' person becomes aware of these people in spirit and this awareness grows as the etheric body loosens its hold on the physical. Very often the dying person will awaken from a sleep and say to those sitting by the bedside, 'I've been talking to Uncle Tom'. Or there may be a staring look as they 'see' someone they thought they would never see again. At the last gasp they may reach out with the arms and have a smile on the face.

These are commonplace experiences and if you discuss them with your friends you will discover many instances that are variations on these themes. What actually happens is that when the spirit leaves the body, and when 'the silver cord is cut' the person is embraced and safely 'carried over'. In common parlance he has gone from earth to heaven.

No-Man's-Land

I want to stick with these old words for a moment. We can carry someone over something, a stream perhaps, or a muddy path. We can think of earth as being on one side and heaven on the other, with some sort of dividing line in between. Let us expand that dividing line into a gap, a gap that in normal death we are carried over by those who have come to meet us. Let us call that gap, no-man's-land, and let us say that this is where dark shadows, lost souls and earth-bound spirits live.

We are actually thinking in physical terms here of course. In reality, no-man's-land would be the second plane, the one above earth which is the first plane. We normally jump over, or rise above the second plane and go straight from the first to the third. Nevertheless, you must remember that the second plane is not another place, it is simply another dimension. Second plane inhabitants are still 'on earth', but vibrating at a higher range of frequencies, though not much higher. The phrase 'earth-bound spirits' indicates that they are near earth but are in spirit.

They are, of course, invisible to us, but only just. Sometimes we can 'see' them, and what do we see? We see a dark shadow. Let us go back to vibrations. Material objects, as we have seen, vibrate at certain frequencies and as we go up the planes so the vibrations become higher. Human eyes are designed to register material vibrations and do not normally register anything higher than that. But the side vision of the eye, which we do not normally use, we prefer to look straight at something to get the best focus and register, the side vision does pick up vibrations in a slightly higher range than the usual material range. Colour comes into the explanation also, from dark, through grey, to white, to brilliance. A spirit near to earth is fairly dark, or at least grey. Now then, how often have you thought you have seen something out of the corner of your eye, but when you look straight on there is nothing there! What has happened is that a spirit has been in your vicinity. Someone who is 'dead' but is still close to earth and is therefore giving off a grey vibration. Your side vision has picked up this vibration and you see a dark shadow. Because you are not sure whether you have seen anything or not, you turn frontal vision in that direction, which cannot register these slightly higher vibrations, and you conclude that as you cannot see anything then there isn't anything there to see!

Incidentally, dogs' ears and eyes have wider pick-up ranges than human ears and eyes. Dogs hear the note of the dog-whistle that is inaudible to us, and they often react to dark shadows that we cannot see.

Of course there are people who have out of the normal hearing, and there are people whose vision does register higher vibrations, who can see spirits. This is a form of clairvoyance.

A ghost, in the popular meaning of the word, is something different. Ghosts are seen by people who are not clairvoyant and they are seen as having a body. This is probably the etheric body which has somehow been able to pick up power from somewhere to keep itself energized instead of dissolving as it should.

In spite of all this terminology, dark shadows, ghosts, spirits, it should be remembered that these are people. When they died something went wrong and instead of making a safe transition, they became stuck in no-man's-land. Remember also that time as we know it only applies to this physical, material world. A person can be stuck in no-man's-land for many years, centuries even; for them, time stands still. This obviously interferes with their spiritual evolution and there is a very specialized branch of healing that we are engaged in, called spiritual rescue, which concentrates on helping such people to get out of no-man's-land and to continue their spiritual journey. There are many such groups, of course, seeking to save that which is lost, but most of you are unlikely to run across them or their work.

I only mention spiritual rescue here in the context of explaining that in healing we are always dealing with people, but not always in the physical sense. Now we must examine how it is that some people manage to arrive in no-man's-land in the first place. Here it may be useful to look again at two of those earlier phrases, earth-bound spirits and lost souls, using the first to describe those who want to be where they are, and the second to describe those who don't know where they are.

Earth-Bound Spirits

These are those who, when they are dying, do not want to die. Do not want to lose contact with earth life. Their attention is fixed on earthly things. They do not see, recognize or acknowledge the spiritual helpers, they die fighting and when they are dead their attention is still concentrated on earth. It is possible in certain circumstances for an earth-bound spirit to impinge upon the aura of a person, rather like a salesman getting a foot in the door, and remain in contact, gradually widening the chink and getting a firmer grip.

We can illustrate this with a rather nasty example. An alcoholic will retain the craving for alcohol after he has died. He may refuse the helping hands that are outstretched towards him on the other side and seek to return to earth for another drink. This he cannot do of course but in time he may find a person of similar temperament and be able to merge with that person's aura. Alcohol tends to destroy one's natural protection and our earth-bound entity may get close enough to be able to obtain some sort of secondhand satisfaction from that person's drinking. It may even get close enough to be able to put the thought into the drinker's mind to have another, and another.

Much the same can be said regarding drug addicts and we have the rather frightening situation where a 'dead' alcoholic or addict can be a contributing factor towards the addiction of someone else.

Mind you, there must be a weakness there in the first place. The door must be opened before the salesman can get his foot in.

You might think that no one in his right mind would willingly invite the attention of an earth-bound spirit, or a lost soul, but in fact many do just that. Consider a group of people playing with a ouija board. 'Is there anybody there?' they call, trying not to giggle. What a marvellous invitation for an entity. Once in, once contact has been made, how can it be broken? The situation needs expert handling. We have had more than one seeker after healing who complained of nerves, bad dreams, etc., and it has turned out that, perhaps years ago, they got involved with a ouija board, something happened and the foot was in the door.

Another way in which an entity can be invited into your life could be through no fault of your own. I have spoken of developing your spiritual qualities and the best ways of doing this are through prayer and meditation. But the wise beginner will not seek to meditate alone. He will join a group or otherwise place himself under the guidance of someone he can trust.

A beginner *is* vulnerable and needs to proceed with caution. It is worth mentioning that there is a difference between spiritual development and psychic development. In spiritual development one lifts one's attention to God and seeks closer union with the Highest. Psychic development may have lesser aims. One may want to develop automatic writing, pyschometry, even fortune telling, purely for amusement or self-gratification. Such situations are tailor-made for the attention of an entity who will certainly be able to gratify your desires, but may also, in time, use *you* to gratify *its* desires. I do not want to frighten you unduly, but at a time when so many people seem to be looking for psychic thrills, a word of warning is necessary. The key to the situation is motive. If your motives are good and pure you will come to no harm.

Lost Souls

Lost souls are often those whose death was sudden and sometimes tragic. The soldier killed by an enemy bullet may be 'living' in an imaginary world of fox holes and snipers. The suicide may be so ashamed of what he has done that he cannot face the Light and those whom he has let down. The motorist killed in a crash may wander through no-man's-land with a sore head not knowing that he is dead. The young mother killed with her child may be frantically looking and searching for the little one. There is no need to fear a lost soul. They will eventually all be found, and in the meanwhile they will do you no harm. It may well be that someone who has experience of healing may read the foregoing and be thoroughly mystified by it all. Well, that is understandable. The spirit friends of a healing group usually deal with the dark shadows, in two ways. Firstly, every team of spirit friends contains 'guardians' whose job it is to ensure that entities do not trespass into the circle of healing light. Secondly, there are always rescue spirits around who will seek to communicate with any earth-bound or lost entity that is attracted by the light, seeking to persuade them to go to where they should have gone when they 'died'.

Spirit Possession

Two final points. The first concerns spirit possession. Be assured that it is not possible for an alien spirit to take over anyone still living on earth. The most that can happen is that an entity can get close enough to put thoughts into someone's mind. But this is interference, not possession. Trance mediumship is, of course, another kettle of fish. There are a number of healers who are entranced by spirit doctors, but even the deepest trance is not true possession, for there is no such thing. It cannot and does not happen.

'Evil Spirits'

The second point concerns 'evil spirits'. When you consider that there are some very wicked people living on earth, it is not hard to imagine that when they die they may refuse to go to the place of light but would prefer to stay in no-man's-land where they will meet with others of their ilk (for like attracts like in the spirit world).

Once there they are powerless to interfere with you or I or anyone else living on earth. We have nothing to fear from them, unless we invite their attentions in ways outlined above.

Evil spirits, in the sense of evil forces, devils, satanic enemies of God, may or may not exist. I would not want to alter your beliefs on the matter, whatever those beliefs may be. If they do exist then they are likely to be engaged in cosmic battle far removed from where you are. In one sense you are not important enough to warrant their attention. But if you ever do find yourself in a situation where you feel that evil is around you, remember this: Good is *always* more powerful than evil, and a cry for help will bring protection. Conquer your fear and trust in God.

We seem to be getting into deep water and straying far from our subject which is, you remember, your healing hands. But we are not really going off course. When you have got to the end of this book you will, I hope, have learnt a lot. You will also realize that there is a tremendous amount that you do not know, for my aim is to spread a wide beam of light on the subject rather than to focus a concentration of light on any one aspect. This means that you learn a little about a lot, rather than a lot about a little.

Indeed it cannot be otherwise, for my own experience has been that we are merely scratching the surface of spiritual healing, and that there is much more that will be revealed to us, as and when we are ready to receive it. Those who are engaged in healing at the present time are still very much pioneers, each new wave of healers is benefiting from the experience of those who have gone before. In our case the only limitations to healing are those limitations imposed by our own minds and our own imagination.

10

CREATIVE IMAGINATION

On a number of occasions I have asked you to use your imagination. To visualize, or picture something in your mind. This creative use of the imagination is a very important activity in healing, more particularly in that part of healing known as absent healing. It is linked with thought and while I want to keep thought and imagination separate if I can, I may not be successful.

Let me talk first about absent healing, dividing it into three parts. Perhaps it should be explained that absent healing is 'sending healing' to someone who is not physically near you, but is separated by distance. The first thing to understand is that distance itself is no obstacle to healing. You can send healing to someone ten thousand miles away just as easily and effectively as to someone in the next street.

Healing in a Group

The first of our three parts is a consideration of a regular healing group that combines contact healing and absent healing. You will remember that when we looked at a typical group meeting we had a period when we sent healing to a number of people whose photographs we had. When a new healing group starts operating, absent healing is likely to be the form of healing that they engage in. They will send healing to anyone whom they know to be ill. Perhaps a little boy down the road has leukaemia. Most of the group may know him and the others can be given the details. After the group has been suitably convened and called to order, the leader may offer a prayer in the suggested manner, asking that the room be sealed and filled with God's loving, healing power. This can be a cue for each member of the group to use the imagination, to *see* the room being filled with golden light. Then the leader may introduce the name of the little boy with leukaemia. Again this is a cue for each member of the group to use the imagination, to build a picture of the boy in his or her thoughts. This is obviously easier for those who know the boy but they can all do it, linking the name with their mental picture.

The next step is to try to visualize the illness. By this I do not mean that you have to know what leukaemia and every other illness 'looks like'. It is sufficient to visualize a 'something' that is wrong, something on which you can focus your thoughts. No sooner have you done this than you begin to build a mental picture of that something dissolving, melting away, being dispelled from the body. You end with a picture of a healthy, happy, smiling boy.

Basically, that is all absent healing is. But it is not 'all in your mind'. By your creative imagination you have 'contacted' the boy and he is as near as you wish. There are refinements to this technique of course. You can visualize a stream of white light travelling from the group to where the boy actually is. A stream of light that carries healing to him. Or you can use your breath as a carrier of healing.

As you breathe in you 'see yourself' breathing in some of the healing light which fills your room, as you breathe out you are conscious of sending that healing-loaded breath towards the boy, bathing him in healing light. As we are now talking about a new healing group you may wonder how they find enough people to send healing to. A little reflection will enable you to realize that there is never a shortage of needy souls. Friends, relatives, neighbours, people at work, the cripple you see whilst out shopping, you will soon have more than you can cope with. Your activities will soon attract attention, from spirit friends who will gather round to help, and from other people who will begin to tell you of someone that they are concerned about. You will soon be marvelling at the many and varied ways in which sick people are brought to your notice.

Organized Church Worship

I said that I would deal with absent healing in three parts. The second part may be restricted somewhat in that it refers to organized church worship. In most services there are opportunities for prayer for the sick, sometimes called 'intercessions', although this term includes all prayers for others. It is not always appreciated that a church service focuses a tremendous amount of spiritual power. Much of this is absorbed by the worshippers, some is used by spirit friends and some should always be used to spread healing. When I am conducting worship I invite the congregation to use their imaginations, in ways similar to those already outlined – visualizing the face of someone they know to be ill, sending a stream of light and seeing them restored to health. In other words, the whole congregation is acting as a large healing group and many remarkable results have come from this.

The third part of this section should be obvious. What can be done in a group or as a member of a congregation can also be done when sitting alone in the quiet of your own room.

Here again it is worth emphasizing that distance is no obstacle. Suppose you receive a letter from your cousin in Australia in which she tells you that she is about to go into hospital for a major operation. You may or may not have a photograph, but you may still remember what she looks like. But if you cannot picture her face, well, at least you have her letter. Just as the paper may hold her latent fingerprints, so both the paper and the words will have her personality stamped on them. Her anxiety will reach to you and you will know that she needs your healing hands. You will send her peace, tranquility, strength of both mind and body and though she be ten thousand miles away, these will reach her as surely as they reach the little boy down the road.

11

THE MECHANICS OF ABSENT HEALING

Once again there are a number of points arising from that last chapter that need to be explained. The first is the question, does it really work? This question may well arise because I brought prayer into the discussion and you may have your doubts about the efficacy of prayer. Well, we shall have a look at prayer later, but first let me deal with the question.

Absent healing may be briefly described as the use of power to make people well. For centuries the same techniques have been used to bring about the opposite effect – to make people ill. I am referring to black magic and other related arts. The black magician, with his wax model and pins, is simply reversing the process of healing. The wax model helps to visualize his victim and the pins help to visualize the pain he wishes to inflict on his victim. You could do this. You could cause sickness and pain, using the methods I have outlined. The strange thing is that many who doubt whether healing works are quite prepared to believe that black magic is effective!

This negative argument does not, of course, really answer the question, and I must confess that the only real answer is that which comes from experience. Over the weeks and months you will gather up strands of 'proof' that will eventually convince that absent healing does work. It is no disgrace to be a Doubting Thomas, and common sense dictates that you should not be gullible; but remember that in the gospel story Thomas asked for proof – and it was given to him. This will happen to you.

To some degree we are all Doubting Thomases, and I suspect that everyone engaged in healing has gone through periods when it seemed that nothing positive was happening. During these times one tends to cling to those strands of 'proof' that have come one's way, and to find them very reassuring. This problem of lack of confidence in what one is doing really springs from a misconception of the part played by the healer in the healing process. As this book is largely concerned with getting rid of misconceptions, it is worth repeating that no technique or ritual, no concentration of effort on the part of the healer can, by itself, bring healing. Healing is subject to natural laws and these should be followed. The healer is in many ways only the last link in the chain. He should accept his place in the scheme of things and not think that he is the be-all and end-all, and that it all depends on him. Nevertheless, doubts can prove to be an obstacle to healing and the mental attitude of the healer should be one of quiet confidence. Alert, yet relaxed, his attitude should be that if he does his lowly task well, then all else will slot into place and healing will come.

Making Contact with Strangers

Another point that needs explaining concerns making contact with someone whom you do not know. Suppose you are asked to send healing to a brother at the other end of the country. We have already said that distance is no obstacle to healing – but how do you contact that person's brother?

Remember the old church idea that every one of us has an 'angel' who watches over us and looks after us? Well, the answer is connected with that idea. I said earlier that none of us is alone, but that there is a spirit friend, a helper, who acts as our 'guardian angel'. Actually it is likely to be someone with whom we have, or have had, a connection, a relative, a favourite aunt or uncle perhaps, but certainly there is someone.

Now then, I am going to explain this rather clumsily. I want you to imagine a rather strange scene.

You and your friends are giving absent healing. 'Up above' your spirit friends are helping. You have this vague information: Mrs Smith's brother who lives across the country. Your spirit helpers send out a general call to other helpers and guardian angels 'does anyone recognize this description?' Of course Mrs Smith's helper is aware that the request has been made and may be able to fill out the meagre information. Eventually the brother's spirit helper replies and says 'Yes, here he is and I am in contact with him'. In this way the full contact is made and your healing thoughts are relayed through the spirit helpers to the man who needs them.

While that may sound very strange, even far-fetched, a little thought may bring to your memory similar happenings: 'I've been thinking about Uncle

George all day. I can't get him out of my mind, I wonder if he is alright?' So you send Uncle George thoughts of concern and sympathy, or perhaps you ring him up or write a letter. What has probably happened is that Uncle George's guardian, sensing that he needed help, sent out a call to those who know him and love him, for help and strength.

Maybe, when you ring him, George tells you that everything is fine, no he is not ill. But it may not be sickness. Perhaps he has a worry at work or a problem that he doesn't quite know how to handle. These things also show in the aura and are picked up as vibrations by his guardian spirit. Does that make sense? I hope so.

The Power of Thought

'Thoughts are things.' As I said before, imagination and thoughts are closely linked together and I was perhaps attempting the impossible in trying to separate them. Anyway 'thoughts' are very important for it is through the medium of thought that most of your healing activities will be conducted. Thoughts precede words for we have to think of what we are going to say before we make the sounds that we call words. No one really speaks without thinking. Thoughts are also the prelude to creative mind pictures and, as will be explained later, these images of the mind are sometimes more useful than words in healing.

Thoughts are real. They continue to exist long after they have apparently gone out of our minds.

Energy or power is needed to create a thought. A man who thinks all day can be just as tired as a man moving bricks. The energy or power needed to create a thought is what makes that thought real and gives it a separate existence. Thoughts which stay in the mind, for instance the thoughts needed to work out a mathematical problem, do not use up as much energy as thoughts which are projected out of the mind, as, for example, when we think of another person. Here the expenditure of power can be quite considerable. A 'good thought', as when we think affectionately of someone, carries power which will do that person good and, conversely, a bad thought will do them harm.

Essentially, of course, thoughts are vibrations and as such we can pick them up. If we are at a crowded football match, the enthusiastic thoughts and hopes of a good result for the home team can become so strong that it will affect all the supporters, welding them together and making them 'all of one mind'.

If we are waiting for a bus on a cold windy day, and the bus is late, the 'irritation' thought may also be picked up by us and we become irritated. We all know that a long wait in a doctor's waiting room can be very depressing. The cause of this is that the waiting room is permanently polluted by thoughts of illness and pain. Dentists' waiting rooms, of course, are filled with fear thoughts and no matter how jauntily we walk in we are quickly subdued as we pick up these vibrations.

Because thoughts are real and thoughts are invested with power they are the best medium for prayer.

Prayer

It is sad that so many of us are brought up to believe that prayers need words – maybe this is one reason why so many give up prayer. Perhaps instinctively we feel that 'saying our prayers' is not the best way. Of course there are many beautiful spoken and written prayers but their main value is that they lead us to *think* about God and about eternal things.

The deep meaning of the Lord's Prayer can never live by our repeating the words parrot fashion, but it blossoms when we let the phrases drift through our thoughts.

Any thought which is an appreciation of the beauties of God, natural beauty, and that which is apparent in love between people, is real prayer.

When we visit the countryside and stop for a moment and take in the scene, trees, grass, sheep on the hills, a bird singing, a lake at the bottom of a valley, and we stretch and smile and think, how lovely it all is – that is real prayer and that thought radiates from us like ripples on a pool.

When we see someone who is sick and we see that this is a disruption of the harmony, unity and rhythm that is God's will, and we say that this should not be, and it evokes our sympathy and compassion, those thoughts, loaded with power, go to that person. This is a healing prayer in the real sense. There is no need to put our hands together or close our eyes or let a word pass our lips.

Once we get used to the idea that good thoughts are prayers we realize that, although we thought we had given up prayer, we have not. We have been doing it all the time. And it is now real and true. With word prayers we tend to fall into a habit of continually *asking* God for things or *asking* God to do something either for us or someone else. With thought prayers we are *involved*.

We can think about life and its problems unhampered by the need to find words to express our thoughts and when we think through to the answer then this is also the answer to our prayer. After all, 'the Kingdom is within' and the God within our thoughts is more real than a God 'up there' who needs to be addressed in a certain manner. The special value of using thoughts to give healing is that we know how thoughts work.

12

THE MIND

In many ways there is a lot of truth in the old saying that it's 'all in the mind'. The mind controls the body as the jockey controls the horse. The trouble is that we can see the jockey but one cannot see the mind. If one were to take a human being to pieces, every nut and bolt so to speak, and lay out all the parts on a table, there would be no part readily identifiable as the mind. There would be the brain of course, and we might be tempted to say that the mind is part of the brain, but it is not as simple as that.

The Conscious and the Unconscious Mind
To understand the working of the mind, as far as healing is concerned, we divide the mind into two parts, the conscious and the unconscious. Metaphorically speaking the conscious mind is the closest to the brain and the body. It is essentially concerned with the physical and the material.

The conscious registers sensory impression. When we taste, see, touch, smell or hear, the nerves in the sensory organs transmit the information to the conscious mind which registers the experience and applies reason and logic to understanding the experience. These two qualities, reason and logic, are the most important contributions that the conscious makes to our life and when we 'think' it is the conscious mind that we think with. It seeks to find a reasonable answer to a situation and a logical answer to a problem – it looks for 'proof'.

There are obviously many situations in life that do not lend themselves to proof and in these the limitations of the conscious mind show themselves. The existence of God is one example. How many of us have thought and reasoned and argued about God? To reason and logic there is no proof that God exists and many people therefore refuse to believe in God. Mind you, the same people may believe in love, may believe that their spouse loves them, although there can be no reasonable or logical proof of this.

The limitations of the conscious mind, mean that it is also the seat of doubt and uncertainty, as well as reason and logic and if the conscious were the only mind that we had then we would quickly go 'out of our minds'.

Links with the Unconscious Mind

However, the conscious mind is only the tip of the iceberg. The unconscious is by far the larger part. The conscious is linked to the unconscious by two paths, two one-way roads.

All the sensory impressions received by the conscious are automatically passed to the unconscious along one of the roads. The conscious is not aware that this is happening: it is an automatic process.

That information is evaluated by the unconscious in the light of greater experience, and the considered opinion of the unconscious is passed back to the conscious along the second road.

There is a difference between these two roads. The first, from conscious to unconscious, is broad and well travelled. The unconscious accepts all the sensory information which is passed to it, even more than the conscious accepts. We can illustrate this by referring to a demonstration often used by hypnotists. A subject is given a sheet of newsprint to look at for, say, fifteen seconds. Then the paper is taken away and he is asked questions about what he has read. As he is using only his conscious memory he quickly runs out of answers. Then he is hypnotized. This time, tapping the unconscious, the subject can produce everything that was on the page.

'Sixth Sense'

We all know that our conscious registers only part of what we see. Many a traffic accident occurs because a motorist looks right and left but does not see all that is there.

Sometimes, however, the motorist gets a kind of feeling to look left and right a second time and is horrified to see another vehicle that he did not see the first time. What has happened here is that the unconscious, receiving the full picture as it were, including the oncoming vehicle that has not registered with the conscious mind, deduces that it is not safe to turn and sends a 'not safe' message along the second road back to the conscious. This is often called 'the sixth sense'. In most people this second road is not nearly so developed as the first and its messages are often ignored. These messages reach the conscious as feelings, intuition, intangible premonitions and are often ignored because they are not 'logical'.

Sometimes we meet someone and form an opinion based on sensory impressions. We form a good opinion and are perhaps ready to accept them at face value, but is there perhaps a little feeling at the back of your mind that he is not all that he makes out to be. 'Nonsense', you say, 'I'm just imagining it.' And we ignore the voice of the unconscious.

Unconscious Memories of the Past
Apart from holding memories of all of this life, the unconscious also holds memories of past lives and takes these into account when evaluating present experiences.

Liken this to a child and an adult. The child tells of its intention to go somewhere or do something. The adult, with greater experiences, may know of some danger or difficulty that may make the adult want to warn the child or suggest a different course of action. If the child ignores this and gets into difficulties perhaps by doing something wrong, the adult will be tempted to say 'I told you so'.

In a similar way the 'adult' unconscious sends its messages of caution. If these are ignored and difficulties arise, there may be a sort of 'I told you so' follow up. This is normally called the Voice of Conscience.

Just as the conscious mind may be called the physical or material part of the mind, linked with the body, so the unconscious can be called the spiritual side of the mind, linked with the spirit and the etheric. It never sleeps, it survives the death of the body and it is open to spiritual influence.

Spiritual Activity during Sleep
The unconscious registers spiritual activity during sleep. It should be understood that when our bodies sleep our spirits often go a-wandering, retaining a connection with the body by means of the silver cord that is referred to in the Bible. These out of the body experiences are necessary, the spirit needs to 'come up for air', as it were.

During these adventures our spirit is 'at home' and we may meet with those who have gone before. A useful by-product of this is that when our bodies die and our spirits are released, they are no stranger to where they are going or whom they will see. That is why dying is so much easier than being born, when we really *are* facing the unknown!

Sometimes it is necessary for our spirit to return to the body suddenly and we wake up with a bump and a feeling of having fallen from a great height. Normally the return is gentle and on awakening some memory of these experiences is passed to the newly awakened conscious mind. Some distortion takes place and the conscious, seeing them as illogical and unreasonable, dismisses them as 'just a dream'.

The Language of the Unconscious

Now then, the unconscious is linked with the spiritual and the etheric and is the guiding intelligence that controls such basic bodily functions as cell renewal. In absent healing in particular, our contact with a person is via his or her unconscious. We cannot do this with words. The language of the unconscious is the pictorial, symbols, pictures and images.

That is why we use imagination and thoughts. As we cannot *tell* the unconscious what is required, we *show* it. We picture what we want to happen and transmit this picture to the unconscious. That is why prayers for the sick do not depend upon words, but upon 'good thoughts'.

Another important point is that while the conscious mind has a ready system of defences and it can accept or reject anything that we might say to the person, the unconscious is to a large extent defenceless to thoughts that one sends its way. It is this natural defencelessness that enables the black magician to do harm – and the healer to do good! Let me hasten to explain that I am not suggesting that the healer forces his will on a poor defenceless fellow being, but, well, a story might explain what I mean.

Someone, talking about a relative who was ill, said to me, 'I'm sure that your healing would help, Mr Blades, but I dare not suggest it as he does not believe in that sort of thing.' Here a direct offer would meet with refusal and a putting up of a conscious mind barrier. But I had no hesitation in agreeing to send him some thoughts (absent healing), knowing that the unconscious would accept my thoughts. It made no difference to me that the subsequent recovery was attributed to the pills he was taking. There is no room in healing for quibbles of that sort.

All this implies that we must be very careful about how we think of people. We should not, on any account, let any thought out of our minds that could harm anyone else. The old saints were right when they spoke of 'sins of thought, word and deed'.

Developing Contact with the Unconscious

It may also be deduced from the above that the two parts of the mind do not always work in harmony with each other. Well, that is true and we would do well to seek a greater co-operation and harmony, for the benefits would be enormous. We can train ourselves to recognize the messages from the unconscious, feelings and intuitions, remember and act upon them, even if at first we cannot see any logical reason for them. Meditation is probably the best way to develop greater contact with the unconscious but, as I have said before, a beginner would be well advised not to try meditation alone but only with an experienced guide.

Seeking to develop contact with the unconscious can, like expanding the aura, attract the attention of an earth-bound spirit or similar unwelcome visitors.

13

SICKNESS AND HEALTH

Although Shakespeare propounded the Seven Ages of Man, an old chestnut amongst doctors is that there are only three ages of man, characterized by the things that claim our interest and attention. Thus the young man is mainly interested in sex, the middle aged man in money and the older man is pre-occupied with his bowels! Maybe there is some truth in that. We do become conscious of the ageing body and its possible malfunctions, whereas the young hardly ever give a thought to sickness. Yet it is in the first half of life that we can create the conditions of later life.

As I said before, the body is important, though not all-important. I likened the body to a motor car, a vehicle which we use during the journey of life. Let us remember that we have a duty to maintain the vehicle in good condition. We can also liken the body to a tool, and as every craftsman knows, you cannot do good work with blunt or mistreated tools.

No, we have a duty to our body, to look after it. There are certain basic rules of health that should be observed, not as a grim discipline, but with natural pleasure.

Sometimes the basic rules are set out as ventilation, irrigation and evacuation.

Ventilation
Ventilation of course refers to breathing and anyone who has ever opened a book on Yoga will know that the Yogi stresses the importance of proper breathing above all else. We normally only use a fraction of our lungs and the unused part acts like a stagnant pool, a good breeding place for germs.

Deep breathing, two or three times a day, keeps the lungs clear. It is strange that so many people will buy all sorts of proprietary concoctions for colds and sneezes but refuse to accept that an alteration in their breathing habits will keep them free from colds for a lifetime. Indeed a lot of sickness arises from bad habits and often the healer has to point out to someone that a change of habit will put their particular problem right.

Perhaps there is a case to be made out for not giving healing to someone who has the answer in their own hands, reserving the healing for those who really are sick.

I would not like to press this but two or three years ago I had an experience that made me think about this matter of personal responsibility to one's body. We had gone to spend the New Year with friends in Northumberland. Arriving a couple of days after Christmas we found our hostess a bit 'out of sorts'. Naturally I offered to give her some healing but as soon as I put my hands on her I got a very clear thought message: 'This is simply the result of too much eating and drinking, I have no sympathy.' Obviously one of my spirit friends took a pretty dim view of our habits, our gluttony, at Christmas.

We were not writing about food and drink but about breathing. It is worth remembering that breathing provides the oxygen that cleanses the blood stream and feeds the tissues. A deficiency here due to our minimum breathing habit can cause all sorts of health problems, particularly if the deficiency is maintained over many years.

Needless to say smoking can exacerbate the problem. The tobacco tars and other nasty substances can collect on the unused part of our lungs. Smokers more than anyone should learn to breath in such a way that the lungs get a good clear out. One last thing: breath through the nose, I know that we can breath through the mouth, just as in emergencies we can be fed through the nose. But the mouth is primarily the channel for food and the nose for air. We do not normally stuff food up our noses, neither should we breath through our mouths.

Irrigation

This refers, of course, to drinking. Water is the only natural drink for humans as for animals, and it is essential that we drink sufficient to keep the system well flushed out. Most of us do not drink enough water and most of what we do drink is infused with drugs as in tea or coffee. There really is no substitute for water.

Evacuation

This is getting rid of waste products. Let's face it, we all tend to eat too much. There is a tendency to look upon obesity as a disease but except for rare cases of glandular disturbance or emotional trouble, obesity is simply due to greed or bad habits. Since we crashed through the standard of living barrier that has made hunger a thing of the past, eating and drinking have become forms of entertainment, and we are forever seeking new ways of dressing up our food and titillating our jaded appetites so that we can eat more and more.

Let us think of our motor car again. We select the right kind of fuel for the engine, and the carburettor meters precisely the right amount for the engine's needs, neither too little (fuel starvation) nor too much (flooding).

Food is simply fuel for the body. If we meter too much the body will store the excess as fat. If we select the wrong grade of fuel (i.e., eat the wrong kinds of food) the performance will be sluggish. Deposits will form and we get constipated.

I once had a hospital appointment concerning some ear trouble. When I reported to the clinic the Nursing Sister asked if I had brought a urine specimen. I told her that I had come about my ears not my water works. 'All systems work together, dearie', she said, handing me a bottle.

And so they do. Good habits concerning ventilation, irrigation and evacuation keep the whole body in trim, whereas bad habits put the complete organism at risk.

Simple natural foods, enough for our needs but no more, will keep us healthy. Obesity, chestiness, and constipation, (leading to arthritis later on) show that we have got the mixture wrong somewhere.

Personal Responsibility for Health

It has been estimated that a quarter of all illnesses results from such bad habits and the healer will frequently be faced with the situation whereby he is asked to help remove the effect when the seeker refuses to adjust the cause. A man asked me if healing would help his wife's weight problem, but if she persists in eating too much then she will continue to get fat. Similarly a heavy smoker who works in a stuffy office, keeps the car windows closed and never gets out and about in the fresh air, is almost certain to develop respiratory trouble. He may ask for healing but what good will come from that if he himself does nothing about the cause? In so many ways the restoration of health involves some kind of change in the life, habits and attitude of the one who has fallen ill. There is a tendency in our time to ignore the personal responsibility for sickness and health and to rely on some sort of pill. To accept illness as something that just happens but will be put right by a doctor. This is all wrong. If I fall ill the fault lies within me. I am surrounded by germs and viruses all the time and they normally do not affect me. When they do, when I develop a virus infection, the fault is in me. What did I do wrong that lowered my resistance and made this attack possible?

I may or may not need a doctor's antibiotics to fend off the invaders, but only I can rebuild the defences, remove the cause and see that such a thing never happens again.

Heart troubles abound in our society but the cause is not in the world, it is in me, in my reactions to activities that I have got myself into. A change of life style is imperative if I am going to restore the harmony of the heart and its essential organs.

There are likely to be cancer cells in my body, and in yours too, but they give no trouble. If, however, they suddenly start to multiply and spread, the main question is, why? What went wrong? Where did I go wrong?

Always the basic cause and the basic cure are with me and in me.

The same source that attributed 25 per cent of illness to bad habits, put the other 75 per cent down to psychosomatic causes – over-stating the case perhaps, because figures like these can never be proved; but the general emphasis is right. Indeed so much illness has been pushed into the psychosomatic tray these days that the emphasis is on asking if there is anything that is not psychosomatic!

Non-physical Causes of Illness

The problem with traditional medicine is that it very often treats the effect and leaves the cause untouched, treating the symptoms rather than that which is causing the symptoms to show themselves. This is inevitable if one is taught and believes that man is simply a body. Doctors are well instructed about the anatomy of the physical body but are not taught about the spiritual realities.

The gradual acceptance that there can be non-physical causes of illness, that the mind can affect the body, is a great step forward, but it is not enough.

We teach that sickness and health are directly affected by the spirit. We erect a sort of hierarchy, with the body at the bottom, the mind above that and the spirit above all. If our body is 'run down' we are vulnerable to, say, virus invasion. If we are mentally 'run down', then not only are we vulnerable to a host of other illnesses, but the body is also run down.

If our spiritual batteries are low then mind and body are affected. Spirit controls and affects everything below it.

We then apply the logical answer – that the cause lies in not only treating the symptoms which show on the lower levels but in re-charging the spiritual batteries, restoring harmony between the divine source and the divine spark. This is the answer to all sickness.

14

WHEN HEALING 'FAILS'

It can be argued that if healing is as simple and logical as I say it is, and if spiritual healing, healing of the spirit by the spirit, is as positive as I claim, then we ought to have a situation in which everyone who is given spiritual healing is going to be cured and the failure rate will be zero. Put like that it reminds me of a television repair man. Faced with a dud set he knows that a short time ago it was working and now a component or a series of components has failed and it is not working. By logical methods he can find and replace the faulty components and then he knows for certain that it will work again. Unfortunately, people are not machines or electrical devices and time and again you will come across instances when the healing that you and your friends are giving, does not appear to be doing any good. And yet there is a dictum amongst healers that healing *cannot* fail! So what has happened?

There is no simple answer to this, mainly because there are many reasons why this should happen and also because no two people are the same. We can give examples of reasons for apparent failure but you may never come across anyone to whom any of these examples may apply.

(1) First of all let us remember that healing can be blocked. A strong negative reaction to an offer of healing will put barriers up which will repel the healing rays. Such a reaction may be against spiritual healing itself as something spooky, weird or otherwise unsavoury. Or it may be a reaction against you as a healer. A sort of 'who do you think you are?' attitude. The best known example of this is told in the Bible. The people of Jesus's home town had this sort of attitude and he was not able to do much amongst his own people.

(2) There are people who expect to be ill, who, in a strange kind of way, enjoy their illnesses. I use the plural because such people usually have more than one thing wrong with them, and if they are cured of one they will quickly develop something else.

Illness becomes almost a hobby and they will swap opinions about pills and potions for all the world like two gardeners talking about soil additives.

(3) Illness can often be a safe way of opting out of a difficult situation. A prop and a crutch that enables us to go slower than the fast moving world demands of us.

(4) We could also include here those maladies resulting from bad habits that we were talking about before.

In these four examples it will be seen that there is no way in which the physical symptoms are going to be relieved quickly. The trouble lies higher up the scale, in the mind, or spirit. Healing will be directed to the cause but it may take years to restore that inner harmony that will provide the strength to bring the lower levels into line. Indeed it may not be completed in this lifetime but may carry on as a hidden weakness into the next.

(5) There are also some physical conditions that are never cleared up but healing gives the strength to overcome and to triumph. This is a reminder that what really happens and what matters in life is the way in which we deal with situations and difficulties. Our spiritual development is the reason for our being here and the triumph over physical suffering and disability largely comes about through seeing them as of no real importance.

(6) A factor in healing which is completely outside of our control, concerns the 'amount' of healing power that is passed through. Once again this can best be illustrated by referring to a car battery.

A flat battery can be charged in three ways. A normally healthy battery that was flattened by persistent use of the starter, can be given a quick high-powered booster charge of short duration. A battery that has been run down over a period of time is best given a slow steady charge over say, twenty-four hours. But a battery that is so low that it is about dead, can only be saved if it is given a trickle charge, when a mere trickle of electricity over a long period, perhaps for a week or more is passed into it.

Sometimes a person's spiritual state is such that it can only be trickle charged. Healing is given regularly over many months before the first signs of response are forthcoming.

The lesson to be learned from this, is that the healer must learn not to look for quick results. I am almost tempted to say that it is none of his business! Often it is only his own ego that wants to see the 'miracle'.

The healer is required to be faithful in little things, and to leave the rest to higher authority. When he has been in healing for a few years he will know that God's way is often slow but sure. He will know that even when nothing seemed to be happening, there was a hidden activity working to a different time scale almost, but certainly working.

(7) Death does not mean that healing has failed.

It often happens that someone will ask for healing as a last resort, when all else has failed and when the doctors have said that nothing more can be done.

Of course books on healing are full of stories where healing has come and the incurable has been cured, but there are obviously many instances where a disease is so far advanced that there is not enough time to reverse the process. When healing is given in such cases it seems to be directed towards two ends. The first is the removal of unnecessary pain and suffering. The body may be breaking up but the pain can and should be eased. A case mentioned earlier of 'M'. She did not need pain killing drugs during her terminal cancer, the healing power prevented pain being felt without dulling her mind.

The second blessing is that the spiritual contacts are strengthened. The healing directs the spirit and the unconscious away from the body, which it will shortly leave, towards the higher planes where the loved ones are waiting.

You will meet many puzzles in healing, but at the end of the day you will agree with me that healing never fails.

15

WHO ARE THE HEALERS?

Time and again in these pages I have referred to 'the healer' – the healer does this and the healer does that. Sometimes when I have done this I have been speaking of myself, telling you of how I do things. Then again I may have had someone else in mind, another healer, one of my friends perhaps. However, as the book has progressed, I have increasingly tried to put you in the role of the healer. I have done this simply because it is my hope that as you read these pages you will become sufficiently interested in spiritual healing to want to take it up and to actually become a healer.

I have tried to whet your appetite by giving you a little knowledge of what I call the mechanics of healing, an understanding of what is actually happening. I have always been interested in the whys and wherefores of the healing that I have done. I like to know what is going on and it is only right that you should also know. The first and perhaps the most important lesson is that there is nothing magical about healing. It is logical, it is natural and it follows easily understood paths.

So this book is in many ways just a taster, a first course. There are other books which will widen your understanding of each and every aspect of the healing process that I have touched upon. All the books that I list in the bibliography have been helpful to me and I recommend them in the hope that they will be just as helpful to you. They are by no means the only ones and you will find as you go along that others are brought to your notice just at the right time when you are ready for the new information that they contain.

If you do decide to take up healing you will be joining a band of men and women that is daily growing. There is a spiritual re-awakening on our doorsteps and healing is doing for people in our time what the outworn doctrines and dogmas of religion cannot do. It is proving, by personal experience, what many people have secretly believed – that there is a God and that God is good.

Nobody really knows how many people are engaged in healing. There is, thank goodness, no regimentation and statistical documentation of healers. My guess is that there are between fifteen and twenty thousand healers currently operating in the U.K., but this is only an arbitrary figure. It may be higher. If we ask who these people are and what they are like, I do not think we are likely to find an answer. If they have anything at all in common it will be those things of which I wrote in the beginning, compassion and kindness, an interest in the meaning and purpose of life and a mind which is open to new ideas and understandings.

What I can say with confidence is that most of them will give their services free to anyone who asks. There are very few professional healers about, although it is reasonable to expect that those who do devote themselves to full-time healing work ought to charge some sort of fee.

On the other hand there are quite a number of healers who, while they do not make a charge, will accept donations, and many of these will use such donations for charitable purposes. As far as my own group is concerned, we have never charged, nor do we accept donations, although we have sometimes had great difficulty in dissuading people from wanting to give us something. Very often they are so grateful for the help that has come to them through us, and this is the only way that they can think of to show their gratitude. I often try to get them to express their gratitude by doing someone else a good turn, buying some flowers for an old lady or something like that. It is generally accepted among healers that as the healing ability did not cost them anything, then they ought not to charge for it. This is a principle that was outlined long ago by the master healer himself, Jesus.

Because healing is essentially a lay craft, involving Mr Average, it follows that most healers follow an occupation of some sort and fit their healing activities in as is convenient. Nevertheless, the two do overlap. On the one hand their healing experiences and training will help them in their daily work. You may remember that I suggested that a healer should be alert and yet relaxed. This ability, practised until it almost becomes second nature, is surely an asset in any occupation.

At the same time while they are at work, they will see and respond to sickness whenever it presents itself. Even the briefest of contacts with someone who is in need, a handshake perhaps or a casual touch and a quick thought, 'healing to this one, please', even that is enough to start the ball rolling.

Giving and Receiving

So we have a principle of giving and receiving. A giving of one's time and energy to healing, and a receiving of a poise and equilibrium that is useful in all of life. This principle of giving and receiving runs right through healing. If I am giving of my services then I receive blessings. In letting the healing power be channelled by me or through me, I receive healing myself, some of it sticks as we say, and a healer can expect that he or she will be blessed with health and strength adequate for the task. Note that phrase, 'adequate for the task'. This does not mean that every healer will be a glowing, bouncing, super-person. Nor does it mean that a healer will never be ill.

This book was begun during a time when I had to call a halt to my own activities because of a sudden attack of angina. Why should this have happened? Should I not have been protected from such a thing?

By no means. I had broken the rules. For a period of some months before, I had been over-working. I had been so busy with this and that and the other that I had been on the go seven days a week almost without a pause. Giving and receiving, I said; but this entails a rhythm, a giving out and then a taking in. After all, if you are breathing out there comes a time when you have to stop breathing out, in order to breathe in! I had lost this rhythm. A number of my parishioners took delight in scolding me for not doing the very thing that I had told them to do. I found out the hard way that what I had told them was true. I soon got over my trouble and I am grateful for the valuable lessons that it taught me. We can always learn more from our mistakes than we can from the things which went right. Sickness can teach us a lot about healing.

Putting myself on one side, there are a number of people whom I know to be doing magnificent healing work, and who themselves have something wrong with them. The very fact that they have intimate knowledge of sickness or of a physical disability makes them more understanding, more compassionate and more useful as healing channels.

There is a parallel in the New Testament. St Paul was a great healer, yet he had some disability that gave him a lot of trouble. Precisely what it was we do not know, epilepsy has been suggested. He did not apparently talk about it very much but simply called it his 'thorn in the flesh'.

Our Average Healer will take a kind of humble pride in his privileged role and will seek to keep himself fit for that role.

If at the beginning of his healing work he has something wrong with him, he may well find that as the years go by that this trouble clears up or is no longer a hindrance to him. He will of course remember what the condition taught him and he will use this to advantage in his healing work. Keeping oneself fit for the healing role is a phrase that has many connotations. In the bodily sense he will refuse to accept infections that less informed individuals might accept as an unavoidable part of every day life.

For example, one person might sneeze and say, 'Oh dear, I'm getting a cold.' Another person, who knows something of healing, might sneeze and say, 'Now where did that sneeze come from? I can't be getting a cold. I don't want one and I'm not going to have one.' So by positive thought he mentally rejects the virus that has come his way. And perhaps he also physically rejects it as he brushes away from his head and shoulders and arms the 'cobwebs' that are loaded with the virus. This, of course, is using the thought control and the creative use of the imagination that has been mentioned in earlier chapters.

These things come automatically to a healer after a time. If it should happen that our healer is off-colour, he will still go along to his weekly healing group meeting. These meetings become very important to us; we look forward to them and feel a sense of loss if the group is not meeting or if circumstances are such that we cannot attend. So our off-colour healer will go along to the group if he possibly can. He may just be a passive participant, and sometime during the evening he will be on the receiving end of healing as the other members of the group use their hands, their hearts and their minds to restore him to fitness.

If, for some reason or other, he is struck down with some more serious illness he will know that he can do as much good from his sickbed as he could when he was hale and hearty. It is a fact, as we all know, that there are many people who, by their attitude during long illness, can be an inspiration and a comfort to all whom they meet. Many a time in the past I have gone to visit someone, perhaps with the thought that I was going to cheer them up, and have come away having been helped more by them than they were by me. Dr William Barclay tells of a visit made by his father, who was also a Church of Scotland minister. He had gone to visit a girl who was suffering from an incurable disease and had taken with him a very lovely little book of comfort written by an anonymous author. He gave it to her. 'I thought', he said, 'that you might like to see this, and that it might help you.' 'I know this book,' she said. 'Have you got it already?' he asked. She smiled and said quietly, 'I wrote it.'

Keeping Body and Mind Fit

In keeping himself fit our average healer will discover for himself a set of basic rules of health, and will do his best to follow them. He may go in for natural foods, 'health foods' or even vegetarianism, but he is more likely to pursue some kind of middle way. 'Moderation in all things' is a very useful motto for a healer. Even the good things of life, when taken to excess, lose their goodness.

Nor will he neglect his mind. That, too, must be kept fit if he is to progress in his healing. Remembering that thoughts are real and that they have life and power, there will be many occasions when he says to himself, 'I ought not to be thinking thoughts like that.' A thought once formed is difficult to destroy and many of us have had the experience of thoughts of the day dream or fantasy type popping up many years after they were first formed.

Ten O'clock Healing

A great many healers will make an effort to join in the ten o'clock healing time. I may need to explain what this is.

During the dark days of the Second World War, when Britain had her back to the wall, one of the little things that welded the British people together was a minute of quietness just before the main news broadcast, the nine o'clock news. Millions of people gathered around their radio sets to listen to news of the fighting and their thoughts would naturally be with those who were dear to them, who were serving in the forces or perhaps in other ways were involved with what we called 'the war effort'. Many a prayer was said, many a tear was shed and this time became a hallowed minute when the mind of the nation was as one.

The ten o'clock healing time is a later version of this. I don't know why the time was changed, although it was probably because the thought emphasis was being changed. However, I do know that many thousands of people sit quietly at ten o'clock, whenever they can, and either send healing or ask for healing, as the case may be.

When we are giving healing to anyone, or even talking about healing, we usually make a point of telling them about this ten o'clock healing time, a time when a tremendous pool of healing energy is formed into which anyone can dip his cup and drink freely.

We are now coming to the end of this little book. Has it been good for you to read it? It is intended to be only an introduction to the subject and its purpose will have been fulfilled if you have come to an understanding that the phrase, 'your healing hands' has meaning for *you* and that through *your* hands, healing can flow.

Some of you will remain unconvinced and will require much more proof than I have been able to offer before they will believe. There is nothing wrong in that, although I would point out that if you are sceptical about healing you may never find proof, but will continually find further grounds for objection. The late Harry Edwards gave evidence to both doctors and clergy about spiritual healing, but failed to convince either. The thousands of case histories in his files were ignored and his invitations to 'come and see' were declined.

See for Yourself
Be as unconvinced as you like, reject everyone's tale of what spiritual healing has done for them, but go and see. The only real and satisfying way for you to obtain proof is the way of first-hand knowledge and experience. Perhaps you might also remember that your sceptical mind is that small part of your mind known as the conscious. Instead of being enslaved by its insistence on impossible niceties of reason and logic, why not listen to the promptings of your unconscious? Do you find that you have a yearning to believe? Do you wish that it was true? That is the voice of the unconscious.

Some of you will have had no difficulty in accepting what you have been reading and may already have taken the first steps in healing. Some may have been surprised to discover that they have already been doing, instinctively, some of the things that I have suggested. This is not unnatural. Healing is a natural activity, and as love and compassion are the only qualifications necessary, it follows that there must be many natural healers happily doing what comes naturally! It is often said that the best possible illustration of healing is when little Tommy, having fallen and grazed his knee, comes in crying. His mother picks him up, she cuddles him, she comforts him and she kisses it better. A perfect demonstration of healing, and nothing could be more natural than that.

Some of you will have tried putting your hands on someone to give them healing and may have experienced a tingling or a feeling of warmth in the hands or fingers. For many people the first confirmation that they can give healing comes when they see tiny flickerings of pale blue or mauve light radiating from their fingers.

Put this book down and try a little experiment. Hold your hands in front of you about eighteen inches away from your face, and with the tips of the fingers touching. Now separate them slightly – can you see a pale light jumping the gap? Probably the best time to try this is when you have just been thinking about healing, or experimenting with the sending of some healing thoughts. As part of these thoughts, imagine that healing power is streaming from your healing hands.

If, no matter how and when you try this experiment, you cannot see anything emanating from your fingers, do not be too disappointed. I never see anything either! Yet I know that healing passes through my hands.

The Potential for Evil

I must add another note of warning. In reading this book you have learned one or two things that are normally best kept secret – the powerful use to which thought can be put, and the creative use of the imagination. I have already mentioned that those people who deal in black magic use these same techniques. You now have these two powerful weapons in your hands. You can use them positively, to do good, or you can use them negatively, to do harm. The warning that I must give is that if you do use these weapons to do harm it will not go unnoticed. The laws of Karma (as you sow, so shall you reap) will ensure that you will have to pay for the harm you do, either in this life or the next time around.

There is in all of us a mixture of good and bad; none of us is all good, or all bad. At every level of life we have to come to terms with these two opposites within. It is generally thought that if we seek to develop the good by becoming more spiritual, then we will rise above the bad and will become all good. Religious and 'churchy' people often think like this, but life is not like that. While it is true that prayer, meditation and good thoughts will help us to rise in spiritual understanding, at every new level that is reached we uncover, as it were, a new level of the bad within us. The brighter the sun shines on our face, the stronger the shadow behind us. A new understanding of spiritual power will release within us the temptation to use that power selfishly, for the gratification of our own ego, instead of in the service of our fellow men and fellow women. The temptation story in the gospels shows that this even happened to Jesus.

16

ODDS AND ENDS

We were saying earlier on that fear is a great obstacle to healing. We had cancer in mind at the time, mainly because the fear of cancer is still very real. Even the word itself is enough to strike terror into the hearts of many. There is no rational reason for this fear. Motor cars are deadly killers but not many people burst into tears when they think about a car. The fear of cancer is related to the memory of people dying slow agonizing deaths. These memories 'live' like a cloud in the atmosphere and they enshroud anyone whose thoughts turn in that direction.

That cloud is very old, but it must be at least forty years since anyone died of cancer like that. Modern drugs have vastly improved the lot of the cancer patient and these days there should be little or no distress, and even the last days of the illness should be pain free.

As we related in the case of M. spiritual healing will often dispel the pain without the need for drugs, although I must admit that M. was a special case. She knew that she had cancer and she also knew the power of healing, indeed she was a healer herself. But her case is a reminder that even the best of us have a long way to go before we attain that spiritual poise that rejects all illness.

I was of course contrasting M. with someone who had not been told that he had cancer. However, while I maintain that it is a great pity that there is that kind of conspiracy of silence, I fully appreciate that while there still remains a great fear of cancer, then it may well be the best course to follow. J. came to us for healing. She said that she was being treated for anaemia and was fed up at having to give up her job and of being tired all the time. In fact she had leukaemia.

She was by nature what might be described as a nervous type and if she had been told the truth about her illness, I think it would have been too much for her. In this case the deception was justified. She responded well to the healing and after about six months she was discharged from medical care as her trouble had cleared up. She returned to work and has had no further trouble.

Whilst a lot of money is still being spent on cancer research, and on trying to isolate a physical cause, the study of cancer as a psychosomatic illness has received much less attention. One notable exception to this is a study undertaken by the Federation of Spiritual Healers. I have no doubt that they would pass on information to anyone who was genuinely interested.

Cancer in young and middle-aged people must always be seen as abnormal and 'wrong', but cancer in old age seems to provide us with a different sort of problem.

Our bodies, after all, only have a limited life and we will all have to say farewell to them someday. Attempts to slow down the ageing process may seem very desirable and a lot of people do want to live longer. But the real question, which nobody asks, is why? What do we want to do with the extra years? Do we want to enjoy ourselves? That is not the best reason! We have certain tasks to perform during this life and the only reason for seeking an extension of the years is surely that we are not yet finished and *need* the extra time. Our rest, our enjoyment, comes when we have finished with this earthly life and have gone home.

Accepting Death

Let me try to illustrate this. An engineer I know was sent abroad to supervise a certain project. He was allowed five years in which to complete it but in fact he managed it in four and was allowed to come home early.

The death of Jesus gives us another example. Many a Good Friday sermon lingers on the 'waste' of Jesus dying at the age of thirty-three, after a ministry of only three years. Crucified in the prime of life, the best years still ahead of him, etc.

But the reality is totally different. He often said that he had a particular job to do and on the Cross he said, 'it is finished', so he went home early.

There is a lot of truth in the old proverb that only the good die young. The secret of life is to know what we have to do, and to do it. When we are finished, then we too can go home. Our earthly age at the time when we go home, the time when we leave our bodies and they die, is immaterial.

We tend to be obsessed by the earthly years. We spend time and money in trying to keep our bodies young. Yet we all recognize the truth in that other old saying that we are only as old as we feel. Not many of us do feel old, the reason being that our real selves, our spiritual selves, do not age, and are nothing to do with the ageing process of the body. While we do have a duty to look after the body, attempts to prolong its life are only sensible if there is a valid reason for needing the extra years.

If there is no such reason and if we are ignorant about what lies ahead and therefore just want to go on living for the sake of living, then it is possible that the break-up of the body will begin before we have left it.

I think I have put that rather clumsily. What I really want to say is that cancer in extreme old age may be 'natural' in the sense that the life of the body has been prolonged too long, rather like a derelict building that should have been demolished years ago. The occupier refuses to move and now the building is slowly collapsing in spite of the attentions of builders who are constantly trying to patch it up.

While I do not want to enter into the debate on euthanasia, I must point out that I have seen many folk who have passed the time when they should have gone to their rest. However, the problem is not solely concerned with the medical attention which keeps their worn-out bodies ticking over. After all, doctors and nurses cannot really do anything else. The ethics of their profession must be upheld. No, the problem is spiritual. There is a lack of teaching, for which the Church must be blamed, on matters which will enable the very old person to recognize when the time has come and to know what to do and where to go.

To return once again to the case of M. I helped her to 'die' in the sense that I helped her to recognize that the time had come for her to leave her body and to go to where her husband and other friends were waiting. 'Come on M., enough is enough. It's time for you to go.'

That is by no means the only occasion on which I have helped someone over the threshold.

The way in which I do this obviously varies with the person, but essentially it includes allaying any fears that they may have, directing their attention to the light and encouraging them to recognize the friendly faces that they can see, assuring them that these are not dreams nor hallucinations.

Roman Catholics may take exception to my remark that the Church fails in its duty to those whose time is near. A priest will usually visit such a person and give 'Last Rites', which in essence are designed to do all that I have outlined. But there is a problem here in that in the hands of an insensitive priest the Last Rites can be no more than a ritual, a necessary formality, a set of words read from a book and lacking in that special 'something' that meets the needs, the varying needs of each individual.

Colour Healing

One final point. It concerns colour healing, a subject that I briefly touched on at the beginning. You may remember that I said that all natural things absorb power and radiate it back again. Flowers do this, and one of the things that we like to do is to send a bunch of flowers to those who have come to us for healing. We probably do this to let them know that we are thinking of them, and no doubt we also hope that the flowers will cheer them up a bit.

In actual fact, because they radiate the healing rays, the bowl of flowers by the sickbed can have a very positive contribution to make towards the recovery of the patient. This can be made even more positive if we send flowers that are of the right colour, that are radiating the kind of rays that the patient needs. For example, if someone has had an operation and needs to regain strength, we can send them flowers which emit strong, powerful rays. The colour for this is red. Any red flowers will do, depending on what is available. As the sick one gazes at the lovely blooms he or she will be absorbing strength, power and vitality.

But suppose another person is suffering from a nervous anxiety type of illness and needs quiet and rest. In this case red would be the wrong choice, it would be too stimulating and might even make the patient restless. Something is needed that will radiate soothing, relaxing, peaceful rays. Blue provides this and this is the colour to go for when choosing flowers to restore peace. Orange and yellow are obviously cheerful colours and flowers in these colours would be a good choice if you want to brighten up a sick room, but if you can find a flower that has a touch of gold in it – then you have a gift fit for a king! Gold is the very essence of healing and in addition a golden flower brings hope, laughter and happiness. It is a strange paradox that this most precious of colours is most often found in the humbler flowers. While we may take an expensive bunch of flowers to our sick neighbour, a child will do more good with an untidy bunch of hand-picked buttercups!

Make sure that your bunch of flowers contains some greenery in it. Green is the divine choice to express harmony and to bring about harmony. Take a walk in the park and see the many, many shades of green, harmonizing perfectly with each other and with everything else that is natural and good. This, you remember, is all about the restoration of harmony, rhythm and unity. Between all parts of the self and between the self and the rest of creation.

FURTHER READING

Cooke, Grace. *Meditation*. 1955.
    Path of the Soul. 1972.
    Both books from the White Eagle Publishing Trust, Liss, Hampshire.
Edwards, Harry. *The Healing Intelligence*: Herbert Jenkins, 1965.
    A searching in-depth study of how healing stimulates the bodily organisms.
    Contains many case histories.
Findlay, Robert. *A Lie in My Right Hand*: Regency Press, 1968.
    The Longest Shadow in the World: Findlay, 1978.
    Two useful books shedding light on how modern spiritual and psychic
    phenomena fits in with traditional Christian belief. The author is a Church
    Elder, a healer and is connected with the Edinburgh College of Para-
    psychology. Both books obtainable from the author, R. Findlay, Boturich,
    Alexandria, Dunbartonshire.
Fortune, Dion. *Through the Gates of Death*: Aquarian Press, 1972.
    Explains what exactly does happen when we die and gives reasons for many
    mourning customs. This book is a must.
Kennedy, Rev. David. *Adventure in Immortality*: C. Smythe, 1973.
    A Church of Scotland minister writes movingly of the communications
    received from his wife Anne over a period of six months after her death in
    January, 1971.
Peddie, Rev. J. C. *The Forgotten Talent*: Fontana, 1961.
Roberts, Ursula. *Letters between Healers*: Psychic Press, 1976.
    A fascinating record of correspondence between the author and three people
    who discover that they have the healing touch. Answers many questions and
    can be referred to again and again.
    Hints for Healers
    Look at the Aura – and Learn
    All three books obtainable from, Miss Ursula Roberts, 7 Sunny Gardens Road,
    London NW4 1SL.
Weatherhead, Rev. Dr Leslie. *The Christian Agnostic*: Hodder, 1965.

INDEX

THE HEALING POWER OF COLOUR

Why do we not like certain colours? Why do men prefer blue and women red? What is your favourite colour and what does this tell you about yourself? **Betty Wood** answers these questions and shows how colour can be used to heal diseased tissue, calm the disturbed, curb vandalism, tempt the shopper and grow super fruits and flowers. We cannot be indifferent to colour — it affects every aspect of our existence — even if we are totally blind. This book will help you to gain an expanded understanding of the nature of colour and how it can be used to enhance your life.